WILLIAMS-SONOMA

Holiday
ENTERTAINING

RECIPES	GENERAL EDITOR	STYLING
Georgeanne Brennan	Chuck Williams	Lauren Hunter
DRINK RECIPES	PHOTOGRAPHY	TEXT
Jordan Mackay	Keller & Keller	Steve Siegelman
	FOOD STYLING	
	Jamie Kimm	

Contents

Welcoming the Holidays   8

OCCASIONS

Gathering for Thanksgiving   26

Gathering for Christmas   40

Gathering for New Year's   54

RECIPES

Drinks   68

Hors d'Oeuvres   90

Soups & Salads   118

Mains   142

Sides   172

Desserts   196

Breakfast   230

Gifts from the Kitchen   244

The Holiday Table   274

Ingredient Glossary   278

Index   282

Think about your happiest holiday memories. Chances are, they are filled with friends, family, and food. After all, the real magic of the holiday season is that it brings people together to enjoy one another's company and the pleasures of the table. There is no better holiday gift that you can give the people you love than providing an occasion for that kind of connection—whether it's a traditional Thanksgiving dinner, a warm, welcoming Christmastime open house, a sparkling New Year's Eve cocktail party, or a cozy Christmas Eve dinner with your family.

This book offers menus and recipes for a whole season's worth of parties, helpful planning guidelines, hosting tips, and easy ways to decorate your home and make your own edible seasonal gifts. You can re-create an entire party menu or mix and match recipes to suit the occasion, your budget, and your own style. The planning, the cooking, and the joy you put into your party will be a gift your friends can cherish all year long.

Chuck Williams

Welcoming the Holidays

This holiday season, you're going to host an enjoyable party or two or maybe even a nice dinner or a casual brunch. And the fun won't be confined to the few hours you spend with your guests. It starts right now, and it will linger long after your party.

As the host, you get to define everything about your party, from the date and time to the guest list and the menu. Before the lights and decorations go up and the world shifts into holiday gear, get out a calendar and start thinking about the kinds of gatherings you would like to have. Minimize your stress by staying realistic, getting organized, and most important, planning ahead. Begin by imagining your party in full swing. Is it dressy or casual? Is it big and buzzing or intimate and relaxed? Will kids be included? For every space, host, and occasion, there's a perfect way to celebrate. Which of the following feels right to you?

a cocktail party Cocktail parties are a festive way to welcome a group of people, and they can be surprisingly easy to host. They have a predefined start and end time, usually lasting a few hours in the early evening or after dinner, so you can serve a few signature drinks and light hors d'oeuvres without having to worry about preparing a full meal. The drinks themselves can be passed, or you can set up a self-service or tended bar.

a casual open house Similar to a cocktail party, a holiday open house lets you invite a lot of people, and it's a good choice when you want to include families with children. Set a start and end time (afternoons work well), and invite people to drop in whenever they can. They will appreciate the flexibility, since they will probably have other functions to attend. You can pass small bites and drinks, or you can set up a self-service buffet of savory and sweet foods (see Hors d'Oeuvres, page 90, and Desserts, page 196), and a drink station, both of which you can restock as needed throughout the party.

a holiday brunch As everyone's holiday calendar fills up, brunch can be a great time to bring friends and family together as well as an easy way to entertain. And if you have holiday house guests, a special brunch will make their stay memorable. Many of the recipes in the Breakfast chapter starting on page 230 can be prepared ahead of time, leaving only a few last-minute details to attend to before your guests arrive. For added ease, set up a brunch buffet on a sideboard and let guests serve themselves.

an elegant holiday dinner The holidays, ranging from Thanksgiving to New Year's, present plenty of opportunities to host a formal dinner party—a great way to celebrate the season with memorable food and a welcoming festive environment. It's also a chance to use your fine china and silver, decorate the house and the table, and prepare a special, multicourse menu to be savored with good wines and good company.

parties of all kinds Once you have cleaned and decorated your house for a holiday gathering, why not host a few other parties to round out the season? There are many types of low-key get-togethers possible. Consider a tree-trimming party with hot cider and snacks early in the season, an informal fireside dinner with your family and closest friends, a casual wine and cheese gathering after work, a cookie exchange, a make-your-own edible gifts party (see pages 244–273), a sweet-and-savory fondue party, a holiday high tea with finger sandwiches and an assortment of Christmas cookies, or a get-together with a fun project, like building a gingerbread house, that involves everyone.

planning the party

As soon as you've decided what kind of party to host, you can start planning the details. At this early stage, keep one important rule in mind: be realistic. The larger the group, the easier and more made-in-advance the food and drinks should be. If you're a busy person, you'll be even busier during the holidays, so keep the preparations and decor simple. Remember, your goal is to be relaxed and ready when the doorbell rings.

where and when

Set a time and date for your event. For some parties, you'll want to specify a time range, usually spanning two or three hours: brunch, 10:00 a.m. to 1:00 p.m.; open house, 2:00 to 5:00 p.m.; tea, 4:00 to 6:00 p.m.; cocktail party, 5:00 to 7:00 p.m. or 9:00 p.m. to midnight. Next, give some thought to the location. Any space can work for a party. Think about creative ways to make the most of your home, such as setting up a bar or buffet on the kitchen counter, or moving the dining-room table next to the fireplace for a cozy dinner. And consider rearranging the furniture for better traffic flow.

guest list and invitations

Write down the names of everyone you want to invite, and then round out the list by adding other people with complementary interests and backgrounds. If you're including kids, invite enough to make up a group. Jot down a few extra names in case you need to invite more people later.

For holiday parties, it's important to give plenty of advance notice. E-mail or call your guests four to six weeks before the party. For formal parties, a written invitation can make the occasion seem more special. Include an RSVP date and contact information.

planning the menu

Once you have an idea of the number of guests you'll be expecting, you can start planning the food and drinks. For inspiration, look over the party menus on pages 18–25. You can re-create them as they are presented, or reshuffle the recipes to make up a menu that suits your style and theme of your party.

the food Begin by thinking about which ingredients are at their seasonal best in your area, and choose recipes that showcase them. You may also want to include one or two favorite family dishes, along with some classic holiday fare, from roast turkey with stuffing and baked ham to pumpkin pie and eggnog. A good menu offers a balance of complementary colors, textures, and flavors. Don't forget to include vegetarian options.

the drinks Sparkling wine is a perfect opener for any holiday gathering. Mulled wine or a festive cocktail is also a good choice. When serving mixed drinks, always offer a nonalcoholic option, served in flutes or cocktail glasses. Special holiday beers from a local microbrewery are another easy, festive option. Round out the bar with still and sparkling water, and be sure to have plenty of ice on hand.

serving and seating

For large sit-down dinners, you can set places at the dining table and serve buffet style from a sideboard or even the kitchen counter. Family-style service (in which the guests help themselves from platters and bowls passed at the table) also works well for this kind of meal. If the group is too large to be seated at the dining table, use the table as the buffet, and arrange for seating in the living room. Restaurant-style service (in which food is served on individual plates assembled in the kitchen) works best for smaller, more formal sit-down dinner parties. Seating should be comfortable and not cramped. If you use benches or wooden chairs, consider outfitting them with pillows.

For cocktail parties and open houses, self-serve appetizer and drink stations work well. If you're expecting a big crowd, it's helpful to separate these stations for easier traffic flow. You can augment whatever you're serving at the stations with passed hors d'oeuvres and cocktails. Hire a helper or ask a friend to assist with serving while you greet guests.

staying organized

Keep a holiday notebook with everything in it, from guest lists and seating charts to photocopied recipes. Make shopping lists for each meal you plan to host and a schedule for each gathering, working back from the start time through the preparations during the days and hours leading up to it. The less you leave to chance, the more relaxed and confident you'll feel on the day of the party.

holiday party calculator

Here's a quick guide to help you estimate party quantities. And remember to err on the side of buying and preparing a little extra.

- Cocktails: 2½ per person
- Wine and sparkling wine: 1 bottle for every 2 or 3 guests
- Beer: 2 or 3 bottles for every beer drinker
- Liquor: 1 quart or liter for every 10 to 12 guests
- Bottled water: 1 quart or liter for every 2 guests
- Party ice: 1 pound per guest; more if using ice to chill bottles
- Finger-food appetizers: 4 to 6 pieces per person per hour
- Desserts: 2 or 3 small pieces per person

stocking up for the holidays

Get a jump on party preparations and impromptu entertaining by shopping for these essentials at the start of the season.

BAR EQUIPMENT

Cocktail napkins, coasters, festive picks and swizzle sticks, corkscrew, bar towels, bar trays, cocktail shaker, shot glass, measuring spoons, ice bucket, wine cooler, tub for chilling bottles, punch bowl, pitchers, carafes

PANTRY ESSENTIALS

Nuts, such as pistachios, almonds, cashews, and walnuts; crackers and chips; cheese straws; bread sticks; assorted mix of olives; mustards; tapenade or other spreads; salsas; smoked fish, such as salmon or trout; caviar; cheeses; chocolates; holiday cookies

decorating for the holidays

Decorate your home at the start of the holidays, and you'll be ready for entertaining all season long. Start by clearing away clutter. Then choose a palette of holiday colors, and add accents in those colors.

trimming the tree A Christmas tree goes a long way toward adding holiday cheer and sparkle. A simple color scheme, such as white lights with ornaments in shades of red and gold, creates an elegant look. Place the tree in a spot that's visible from many angles and out of the way of foot traffic, the fireplace, and heaters. Test the lights first, and then string them on the tree, starting at the base of the trunk and working your way out and up, before placing the ornaments.

creating a mood with light Lighting can give any space an instant makeover. Begin by turning off or dimming all overhead lights in the rooms in which you will be entertaining. Keep unused rooms dark. Next, add warm accent lighting with floor and table lamps. String strands of miniature white Christmas lights along the mantel, on banisters, or along molding or baseboards. Arrange pillar or votive candles on the mantel, buffet, and dining table and throughout the space to create soft, flattering light. Keep candles a safe distance from food or anything flammable, and out of the way of guests.

styling the table To give the dining or buffet table an attractive holiday look, start with a white or solid-colored tablecloth or a bright, festive table runner. Set the table with your good flatware, dishes, and glassware, and then add a few colorful accents to each setting, such as a folded napkin, a sprig of holiday greenery, salt and pepper cellars, a place card, and a party favor.

styling with flowers Visit a flower market or farmers' market, where you can buy boughs, wreaths, and garlands of greenery that will stay vibrant throughout the holidays, such as pine, spruce, holly, cedar, or eucalyptus. Stock up on floral supplies, including wire, tape, and foam, as well as gourds, pinecones, seasonal fruits, sprays of red and white berries, colorful leaves, and other natural items for decorating.

scents of the season

If you have a fireplace, light a fire just before the guests arrive and throw in some pine-scented incense. Put a pot of cider or wine with mulling spices on the stove just before the party, so its aroma fills your house. Place candles with seasonal scents, such as pine, cinnamon, and vanilla in the entryway, bathrooms, and family room. Avoid placing scented candles near the dining area, so they don't compete with the aromas of the food.

music sets the mood

Gather your favorite holiday CDs or make playlists ahead of time. Start with mellow music to welcome the guests; increase the volume and energy level once the party is in full swing. Create a couple of quiet conversation areas for guests who don't want to talk over the music.

holiday garnishes

Here are some easy-to-find garnishes for making food more festive.

greenery Arrange sprigs of fresh herbs, such as rosemary, sage, mint, or parsley, in a cluster at one end of the platter or on each guest's plate.

seasonal fruit and nuts Rim the edge of the platter with miniature apples, cranberries, kumquats, grapes, walnuts or almonds in the shell. You can use these in combination with fresh herbs to create a wreath effect.

pomegranate seeds Sprinkle a handful of pomegranate seeds on or around roasted meats and other foods, especially those with sweet-savory flavors.

mint sprigs Keep fresh mint on hand for garnishing just about anything sweet. Place a few red berries alongside the mint for added holiday color.

candy Use white and dark chocolate truffles, candy canes, or peppermints to decorate dessert plates and platters.

autumn

acorns, **apples**, bittersweet, **chestnuts**, maple leaves,
olive branches, persimmons, **pumpkins**, quinces,
rosehips, squashes, **walnuts**

amaryllis, citrus, cyclamen, holly, magnolia, narcissus, pears, pepper berries, pine, pomegranates, seeded eucalyptus, tallow berries, winterberries, white fir

holiday planner

november

Thanksgiving dinner is often the most elaborate meal you'll prepare all year. The secret is to start planning early in the month so all of the details are worked out ahead of time.

EARLY Make a guest list and invite everyone. Start planning the menu and making shopping lists. Order the turkey. Count dinnerware, glassware, linens, utensils, and serving pieces, and buy what is missing.

MID Confirm the number of guests and assign them any food items to bring. Buy wines, beverages, and candles. Arrange for any fresh or prepared foods. Order flowers and decide on your centerpiece.

LATE Iron table linens. Pick up the turkey. Set the table, make the centerpiece, and start cooking a day or two in advance.

december

This is the most social month of the year. Get a jump on holiday hosting by shopping early and readying your home for entertaining in a single burst of creative energy.

EARLY Plan occasions and invite guests. Stock up on holiday essentials (page 11). Purchase or make holiday cards and shop for gifts. Buy and trim the Christmas tree. Hang your holiday lights and decorate with greenery and candles.

MID Mail your cards and gifts. Choose table linens, china, and silverware, and iron or polish as needed. Plan your menus, make shopping lists, and order your ham, turkey, or special foods.

LATE Select seasonal music and assemble your holiday centerpieces. Make holiday cookies, edible gifts, and party favors.

thanksgiving feast

serves 10 to 12

TO START
Apple Cider Cocktail, 86

Cheese Straws with Sesame Seeds, 94

ON THE BUFFET
Roast Turkey Seasoned with Sage, 158

Mashed Potatoes and Celery Root, 178

Green Beans with Bacon and
Onion Vinaigrette, 185

Gingered Cranberries, 188

Maple-Thyme Biscuits, 191

FOR DESSERT
Pumpkin Pie with Walnut Crust, 210

Wine Suggestions
For a white, serve a Sauvignon Blanc or
California Chardonnay, and for a red, serve
a Côtes du Rhône or Zinfandel.

elegant thanksgiving

serves 6 to 8

TO START
Camparini, 85

Warm Citrus Olives, 103

AT THE TABLE
Butternut Squash Soup with Ginger
Crème Fraîche, 120

Radicchio Salad with Pears, Walnuts,
and Goat Cheese, 133

Grilled Turkey with Maple Glaze, 162

Brussels Sprouts with Shallots
and Parmesan, 186

FOR DESSERT
Cardamom Crème Brûlée, 202

Wine Suggestions
For a white, serve a Viognier or Grüner Veltliner,
and for a red, serve a Pinot Noir or Syrah.

small thanksgiving

serves 4 to 6

TO START
Lillet Cocktail, 85

Dates Stuffed with Fontina and Hazelnuts, 99

AT THE TABLE
Turkey Breast with Chorizo, Oregano,
and Peppers, 157

Roasted Squash with Maple Syrup
and Sage Cream, 180

Rosemary Popovers, 192

FOR DESSERT
Cranberry and Pear Crisp, 220

Wine Suggestions
For a white, serve a Viognier or Chardonnay,
and for a red, serve a Tempranillo or Dolcetto.

weekend breakfast

serves 4 to 6

RECIPES
Frittata with Spinach, Roasted Red Peppers,
and Gruyère, 233

Sausages with Sautéed Apples and Onions, 236

Twice-Cooked Potatoes with Fresh Herbs, 237

Cranberry Cornmeal Muffins, 241

holiday tea

serves 8 to 10

RECIPES
Smoked Salmon Canapés with Caviar, 111

Buttermilk-Blueberry Scone Bites, 240

Caramel Sea Salt Truffles, 258

Fig and Walnut Quick Bread, 261

cookie exchange

serves 8 to 10

RECIPES

Coconut Macaroons, 253

Chewy Ginger-Molasses Cookies, 260

Chocolate-Peppermint Crinkles, 264

Sugar Cookies, 256, with Royal Icing, 257

Lemon Zest Shortbread, 251

holiday breakfast

serves 6 to 8

RECIPES

Hot Rum Coffee, 74

Grapefruit Compote with Fresh Mint, 232

Scrambled Eggs with Mushrooms,
Cheddar, and Pancetta, 235

afternoon buffet

serves 8 to 10

TO START

Crunchy Sweet Potato Chips, 97

Caramelized Onion and Sour Cream Dip, 97

ON THE BUFFET

White Bean Soup with Rosemary, 121

Watercress Salad with Apple, Celery,
and Blue Cheese, 134

Baked Ham with Spiced Cider Glaze, 166

FOR DESSERT

Rich Chocolate Brownie Cake, 221

Wine Suggestions

For a white, serve a Riesling or
Gewürztraminer, and for a red, serve a
Brunello, Syrah, or Zinfandel.

wine & cheese gathering

serves 6 to 8

ON THE TABLE

Dates Stuffed with Fontina and Hazelnuts, 99

Antipasto Classico, 104

Winter Cheese Plate, 198

FOR DESSERT

Pumpkin Pie with Walnut Crust, 210

Wine Suggestions

For a white, serve a Chardonnay, Friulano,
Sauvignon Blanc, or sparkling wine, and
for a red, serve a Sangiovese or Pinot Noir.

fondue party

serves 4 to 6

TO DRINK

French 75 Champagne Cocktail, 73

THE MAIN MEAL

Mixed Greens and Fennel with
Ricotta Salata, 130

Artisanal-Cheese Fondue, 102

FOR DESSERT

Blood Orange Granita, 227
Lemon Zest Shortbread, 251

Wine Suggestions

Serve a white such as Grüner Veltliner,
Sauvignon Blanc, or sparkling wine.

casual dinner

serves 4 to 6

TO DRINK

Ruby Red Grapefruit Martini, 82

ON THE BUFFET

Mixed Greens and Fennel with
Ricotta Salata, 130

Risotto with Porcini Mushrooms, 144

FOR DESSERT

Cinnamon Coffee Bundt Cake, 242

Wine Suggestions

For a white, serve a Friulano,
Verdicchio, or Soave, and for a red,
serve a Merlot or Barbera d'Alba.

family gathering

serves 4 to 6

TO START

Cranberry-Lime Punch, 81

Three-Spice Chex-and-Nut Mix, 98

Baked Goat Cheese with Honey
and Apples, 103

THE MAIN MEAL

Leek Soup with Pancetta
and Bread Crumbs, 127

Tarragon-Stuffed Chicken with Pan Gravy, 156

Glazed Parsnips and Carrots with Sherry, 177

Cauliflower Gratin, 182

FOR DESSERT

Latticed Apple Pie, 209

Wine Suggestions

For a white, serve a Pouilly-Fuissé,
or Sancerre; for a red, serve a Beaujolais,
Chianti, or Côtes du Rhône; or serve a rosé.

midwinter dinner

serves 6 to 8

TO START
Pinzimonio, 104

THE MAIN MEAL
True Cod Fillets with Shallot
and Meyer Lemon Sauce, 148

Spicy Braised Escarole, 187

Root Vegetable Purée, 175

FOR DESSERT
Almond Pound Cake with Cherry Glaze, 206

Wine Suggestions
For a white, serve a Pinot Grigio
or Riesling, and for a red, serve a
Tempranillo or Zinfandel.

holiday cocktail party

serves 10 to 12

TO DRINK
Lemon Verbena Drop with Thyme, 82

Ruby Red Grapefruit Martini, 82

TO PASS
Cucumbers with Pickled Ginger and Crab, 108

Ricotta-Stuffed Cherry Tomatoes, 100

Endive with Gorgonzola, Pear,
and Walnuts, 100

Filet Mignon Skewers with
Balsamic Reduction, 117

TO FINISH
Ice Cream Truffles, 228

Gathering for
Thanksgiving

More than any other holiday, Thanksgiving is the great American feast. Make the celebration as casual or elegant as you like, regardless of how many are around your table. Think of it as an abundant meal that reflects your generosity and personal style, a perfect occasion to mix and match heirloom servingware with modern pieces and family favorites with contemporary recipes.

To mark the holiday, decorate your table with autumnal touches. Even the simplest arrangement of candles or flowers creates a welcoming mood, giving the people you love something to be truly thankful for: a chance to share life's bounties together and a meal to remember.

planning ahead

The real work of Thanksgiving is more in the preparations than in the event itself. Order a high-quality fresh turkey several weeks in advance, if you can, and begin planning the menu at the same time. To round out the meal, choose simple, special foods you love to make without taking on too much. Asking friends to bring something, such as wine or a pie from a bakery, takes pressure off of you and gives everyone a chance to participate. Try out any new recipes ahead of time, so you get a sense of both timing and flavor.

setting the table

Well before the holiday, take stock of your platters, bowls, linens, flatware, and tableware so you can borrow, rent, or buy whatever is missing. Set out platters on the buffet to see how everything will fit. Look over the guest list and create a seating plan, then check to see that you have enough comfortable chairs to fit around the table. During the days before the holiday, give some thought to the table centerpiece and other decorative touches, such as place cards and a creative napkin fold, that will make the table feel festive and welcoming.

serving the meal

Set out light snacks, such as olives, nuts, fresh vegetables and dip, or a simple antipasto platter (page 104), so guests will have something to nibble on as they mingle over drinks before sitting down for the meal. Have sparkling cider on hand for the kids. Thanksgiving is an ideal occasion for setting up a buffet and having guests help themselves to as much food as they want. If you decide to serve family style and pass platters at the table, it's helpful to set up a sideboard or serving table for setting the platters on when they're not being passed. Whichever service you choose, it's a nice touch to present the turkey or ham whole, with the host carving and serving each guest from the head of the table or at the buffet.

at the celebration

- Welcome guests with a tray of prepared drinks with festive garnishes.

- Use cloth napkins that complement the table setting. Fold or tie them with a decorative element, such as foliage from the centerpiece or even bread sticks or cheese straws.

- For an intimate gathering, serve the meal on the kitchen table or a table set up beside the hearth.

- Use a mix of contemporary serving dishes and traditional or antique pieces.

- Pass bread on a rustic cutting board or in a linen-lined basket.

- Have some games, toys, and movies on hand if you're inviting families with kids.

in the kitchen

- Prepare cranberry sauce, relish, or chutney up to two weeks ahead of time and store tightly covered in the refrigerator.

- To save time at the last minute, prepare gravy in advance, making it a little thicker than usual; reheat and thin with water just before serving.

- While the turkey or ham rests, reheat and plate the side dishes, cover with aluminum foil, and place them in the still-warm oven until serving time.

- If carved turkey meat looks dry, moisten it just before serving by sprinkling it with a little hot chicken or turkey stock.

The Thanksgiving Centerpiece

1 Gather the elements: A purchased wreath made of olive branches, laurel, rosemary, or evergreen boughs (a square wreath makes an attractive centerpiece); cream-colored pillar candles; bittersweet or other berry vines or dried foliage; and amber-colored glass vases, bottles, or carafes in pleasing shapes. Keep the palette soft, natural, and autumnal.

2 Assemble: Place the wreath in the center of the table. Space the pillar candles evenly around the inside edge of the wreath, and put a cluster of vases in the center. Arrange sprigs of foliage, berries, or vines in each vase, using only a few branches to keep the look light and airy and to avoid blocking sight lines across the table. Make a similar, smaller arrangement for the buffet.

continuing a theme

When arranging the centerpiece, think about related accents and touches, such as amber-colored water glasses or carafes, that will pick up the tone of the vases, creating a pretty visual pattern around the table. Carry the design through the house by using the same types of candles, vases, and foliage to decorate the mantel, sideboard, and occasional tables.

More Ideas for Thanksgiving Centerpieces

acorn pedestal

Buy natural-themed ornaments made from twigs, acorns, and nuts, or use pinecones, gourds, or dried seedpods. Wrap each in a velvet ribbon and arrange in a wooden or ceramic footed dish.

harvest bouquets

Use autumn foliage, such as tea roses, seeded eucalyptus, or fresh or dried hydrangea. Gather small patterned or plain bowls in dark natural tones and place floral foam or a frog in each. Trim foliage one piece at a time and insert, starting at the center, to make a low, full domed shape.

persimmon bowl

Arrange persimmons in a footed amber glass dish or bowl. Cut sprays of autumn foliage and insert cut ends between the persimmons. You can also use tangerines, miniature apples, or small gourds.

Ideas for Thanksgiving Place Settings

harvest paper wraps

Cut or tear strips of seasonal wrapping paper in shades that complement your napkins. Wrap around napkins, twisting to secure it on the underside, and slide flatware under the loop. Place on or beside each plate.

natural stars

Buy star anise pods at any specialty grocery store. Fold pretty linen napkins to make squares, place on plates, and arrange a few pods on top. You can also use miniature pinecones, acorns, seedpods, or a few small autumn-colored leaves.

pumpkin place cards

Use a metal skewer to carve guests' initials on miniature white or orange pumpkins. You can also use a white or metallic marker to write initials or names. Set a pumpkin on or above each plate.

nut cups

Welcome guests to the table with an edible decoration. Fill small dishes with in-shell or shelled nuts, olives, or tiny crackers. Add strips of paper with guests' names to the dishes for place cards.

Ideas for Lighting Up the Thanksgiving Holiday

glass vases with organics

Place stocky pillar candles or votives in small, low glass vases of different shapes. Use rice, sand, pebbles, seeds, beans, or cranberries to anchor the base of each candle. You can cluster vases of different heights to make a pleasing arrangement, run them in a line down the center of the table, or set them out singly or in groups throughout the house.

ribbons and natural touches

Buy different patterned ribbons in fall colors that complement your table and decorating palette. Wrap lengths of ribbon around candles, securing ends on the underside with double-stick tape. Group candles on rustic plates or trays and finish each arrangement with a few acorns, fall leaves, seedpods, pinecones, or a mix of elements.

Gathering for
Christmas

The weeks leading up to Christmas provide all
kinds of opportunities for hosting everything
from elegant dinners to open houses. A Christmas
Eve dinner, Christmas morning breakfast after
the gifts are opened, and meals throughout the
holiday weekend are all ideal occasions for intimate
get-togethers with family and close friends.

The key to entertaining during this busy time,
and making your home warm and inviting, is
to stay realistic and true to your own style. Plan
menus that are seasonal and unfussy, and keep
decorations beautiful and natural. Then light up
the tree, fill the house with greenery, candles,
and holiday music, and you're ready for anything.

planning ahead

Start thinking about how you want to celebrate Christmas several weeks before the holiday. If you are hosting more than one gathering, draw up a guest list for each, as well as lists for food, drinks, and decorations. Planning all of your Christmas entertaining at once in this way allows you to look for opportunities to double up on food and decorations and makes the preparations more efficient. Order special items like prime rib and wine ahead of time. Stock up on colorful Christmas napkins for cocktails and appetizers, snack foods, and party ice. Plan games or activities for kids and rent or buy some Christmas movies to show.

setting the table

Check your supply of linens, glassware, flatware, and serving dishes in early December and note anything you might need to buy, borrow, or rent. Polish the silver and wash glassware that has been in storage. The night before a party, iron the table linens, and set up the table or buffet. Take care of details ahead of time, such as lining the bread basket with a linen cloth and setting out butter dishes, salt and pepper cellars, gravy boats, and pitchers for water and drinks. Use silver, gold, and crystal accents to create a sparkling mood.

serving the meal

The hour before the meal can be stressful as people begin to arrive and you're dealing with final preparations. Make it easier by welcoming guests with simple drinks and made-ahead nibbles. Once guests have been greeted and are mingling, give yourself 20 to 30 minutes in the kitchen to pull together the food and arrange the meal. The larger the group, the less complicated your serving style should be, with buffet or family style the easiest. A self-serve drink station is always a good idea for large gatherings, from an open house to a sit-down dinner. Hire a helper or enlist a family member or friend to help keep the bar stocked with drinks and ice throughout the party.

for the celebration

- Use a rubber stamp with a whimsical or seasonal design and metallic ink pad to print your own place cards, writing guests' names on each with a matching metallic pen.

- Instead of a traditional place card, use a small wrapped gift or a Christmas ornament with the guest's name and the date written on it, or a mini bouquet of holly.

- Use candles for daytime Christmas celebrations, too. They'll add sparkle even on a bright winter day.

- Set up everything you need ahead of time for making and serving coffee, tea (caffeinated and herbal), and cocoa.

- Finish the holiday meal with chocolates, cookies, or a cheese plate (page 198) and espresso and cordials.

in the kitchen

- Clean out your refrigerator and freezer during the week before the holiday, so you have plenty of room for party food.

- During the hours before the party, clean as you work, so that the kitchen is in order when the guests arrive.

- Post the menu, copies of recipes, and to-do lists in a central spot in the kitchen, so you can easily check them throughout the party.

- Choose dishes that can be made in advance and reheated or finished simply at the last minute.

- Set out ingredients for any last-minute cooking in bowls, grouped together on trays, so you don't waste time searching for them during the party.

The Christmas Centerpiece

1 Gather the elements: A long, narrow white ceramic or clear glass platter or tray; small red and clear glass bud vases (choose different shapes or a use a matching set); stems of small white flowers, such as ranunculus or freesia, and red flowers, such as amarylis or roses; and ferns or other greenery, such as pine.

2 Assemble: Put a little water in each vase, and trim the stems of the flowers and greenery so they sit snugly on the rim of the vase. Add one or two blooms or a stem of greenery to each vase and line them up on the platter, varying colors and heights. Or, place a single vase at each place setting or elsewhere in the house.

continuing a theme

Buy extra-long, thin tapers in white, cream, red, or green. Melt the candle bases slightly and affix the melted ends on the bottoms of small, decorative bowls, spacing the candles evenly to create an airy arrangement. Fill the bowls with miniature Christmas ornaments, pebbles, marbles, in-shell nuts, or cranberries.

More Ideas for **Christmas Centerpieces**

tray of red pears

Seasonal hard fruits and loose greenery make a simple, striking centerpiece. Use any variety of pear or apple, or pomegranates, combined with sprays of seeded eucalyptus, pine, or fresh herbs such as rosemary or thyme. Arrange the fruit on a tray, platter, or bowl, tuck the greenery in between, and surround with votives or tea lights in complementary hues, like blush mauve and sage green.

red flower burst

Floral arrangements featuring a mix of blooms of a single color are dramatic and unexpected. Here, Christmas red tulips and ranunculus are combined to make small arrangements in red ceramic bowls. White flowers in white bowls also create an elegant, festive effect for Christmas or New Year's. Cut the stems short and use floral foam to anchor the blooms, making a tight dome of flowers. Place multiple bowls or vases along the dining table, mantel, or sideboard.

Ideas for Christmas Place Settings

berry spray

Lay a sprig of rose-hued pepper berries, rose hips, or witch hazel on each plate. Use some of the same foliage in the centerpiece and in other decorations throughout the house.

napkin bouquet

Any combination of seasonal berries or small flowers, mixed with greenery that has a strong graphic shape, works well for a mini bouquet to mark a place setting. Here, white tallow berries (ideal for centerpieces and wreaths as well) stand out against a fan of sage leaves. Form a small cluster of berries and leaves, tie with a velvet bow, and place on each napkin or above each setting, adding a name card if you like.

pomegranate place card

Hearty fruits (and winter vegetables) are a whimsical way to mark a place setting. Buy a few dozen pomegranates, apples, pears, quinces, or persimmons, selecting fruits that are small and unblemished (you can arrange extras in a pretty bowl). Write each guest's name on a strip of card stock, vellum, or other decorative paper. Using a paring knife, make a small slit in the top of each fruit and insert the name card. Place a fruit on each napkin or above each place setting.

Ideas for Lighting Up Christmas

vintage glasses with berries

Small cordial glasses, antique juice glasses, or shot glasses double as votives and miniature vases. Gather the glasses and then select berries (such as hyperican berries) and candles that match or complement their color. Delicate flowers also work well. Fill the glasses with water and float a tea light in some (use tongs to put in place) and arrange berries or flowers in others. Group a cluster of the glasses, mixing votives and vases, on a tray. For an added flourish, scatter small pinecones or nuts on the tray.

ornamented candles

Use long lengths of raffia, jute, or fine ribbon to attach flat Christmas tree ornaments to pillar candles. Choose colors such as silver or gold for extra sparkle, or use sprigs of evergreen (or try pine or spruce). Surround the base of each candle with evergreen boughs and natural red accents, such as winterberries or holly berries.

Gathering for
New Year's

For just about everyone, New Year's is all about socializing. And that makes it the ultimate holiday for having people over. You might want to invite friends to a dressy New Year's Eve cocktail party, a sit-down dinner with a festive menu featuring special wines and decadent desserts, or a laid-back open house on the first day of the year.

Whatever your entertaining style—elegant or casual, intimate or standing room only—hosting a New Year's party can be an ideal way to connect with the people whose company you enjoy, return a year's worth of invitations, and get a jump start on that perennial New Year's resolution: having friends over more often.

planning ahead

Order wine, liquor, bottled water, mixers, soft drinks, and party ice in advance, and have them delivered to your house to save time. Consider buying a case or more of sparkling wine. Rent or buy enough Champagne flutes and cocktail glasses to serve everyone. Since most stores close early on New Year's Eve, do your shopping ahead of time. Order specialty items, such as caviar and cracked crab, in advance and ask if they can be picked up early in the day.

setting the scene

Make or buy invitations that establish the look and color scheme of your gathering. Stock up on candles of varying shapes and sizes to supplement your holiday decorations. They'll add a glamorous glow to evening parties and a cheery mood to daytime gatherings. Use light-colored table linens and decorate with silver, stainless steel, chrome, gold, and glass accents—including candelabras and trays, ribbons, metallic ornaments, and balloons—to create a glittering effect. Use white flowers to create decorative arrangements. Give Christmas greenery a New Year's look by swapping out red accents and replacing them with silver or gold items.

serving the food and drinks

Serve finger food and cocktails on trays and platters lined with linens, so the color of the food and drinks stands out. For cocktail parties and open houses, serve a mix of passed hors d'oeuvres and an assortment of self-serve appetizers arrayed on a buffet, coffee table, or kitchen island. Chill sparkling wine and welcome guests with a tray of filled flutes. For large groups and cocktail parties, prepare the bar and set out coasters and trash receptacles early in the day. You can also set up a satellite self-serve drink station with wine, beer, and soft drinks in another part of the space to help party flow. If gathering in the living room, light a fire in the fireplace and decorate the mantel with candles to add sparkle.

Come Join Us
To Celebrate
The New Year
Sunday, January 1
3 to 7 PM
All Ages Welcome

for the celebration

- Set out stacks of cocktail napkins at each food station. Use cloth napkins rather than paper for a more elegant look.

- Use votives in clear, faceted glasses and white blooms to decorate the table and the space.

- Present drinks in a festive way, such as tying silver or gold curling ribbon around the stems of flutes and cocktail glasses.

- Light a fire in the fireplace before the guests arrive and have extra logs on hand (recruit a guest or family member to tend the fire throughout the party).

- Offer ginger ale, sparkling cider, or grape juice in flutes as an alternative to sparkling wine, as well as a special nonalcoholic mixed drink.

in the kitchen

- Finger-food items should be made in advance and either ready to serve or assembled with minimal last-minute effort.

- Post a chart showing heating times and assembly instructions for various hors d'oeuvres.

- Keep hot appetizers warm in a low (250°F/120°C) oven on aluminum foil-lined baking sheets.

- Make back-up platters of buffet items so you can swap out the entire platter when the quantity is low.

- Prepare simple garnishes for trays of hors d'oeuvres to be passed ahead of time, such as small bouquets of herbs, flowers, or citrus.

- Designate a time when you will switch out the buffet or passed items for desserts.

The New Year's Centerpiece

1 Gather the elements: Flat glass bowls or low, footed glass candy dishes (you can use matching ones, or vary their heights and shapes); white roses or other flowers, such as ranunculus, chrysanthemums, tulips, or freesia; and flax leaves, ferns, or palm leaves (available at florists or wholesale flower markets).

2 Assemble: Coil a few flax leaves around the inside edge of each dish to make a border. Trim the flowers, leaving about 1 inch (2.5 cm) of stem attached, and arrange inside the leaf border. Add a little water to each arrangement. Place along the center of the table and as accents throughout the space.

continuing a theme

To pick up the natural green and white look of
the centerpiece, tear some flax leaves into strips
that are ½ inch (12 mm) wide and use them to
tie flatware bundled in napkins for the buffet or
dining table. You can also use the leaves to dress
up glasses, wrapping them around the glass and
tying them in place with raffia.

Ideas for New Year's Decorations

pussy willow sprays

Buy pussy willow stems and sphagnum moss from a floral shop. Use floral foam or a frog to anchor the stems in low ceramic vases, bowls, or watertight wooden boxes. Add a small amount of water. Pack moss around the edges of the arrangement to help hold stems in place and conceal the foam.

spider mum sparklers

Gather several small vases or Asian-style teacups. Cut white spider mums into short lengths, so that the flowers sit just above the rim of the vases. Fill each vase half full with water and place a flower or two in each, along with sprigs of fresh laurel and seeded eucalyptus. Group several vases to make a centerpiece, or put one at each place setting.

citrus starbursts

Use lemons to make a colorful, fragrant centerpiece or side-table arrangement. Insert whole cloves into some of them to create whimsical patterns, such as spirals. Attach star anise pods to others by tying them in place with raffia or twine. Line a pretty white dish or shallow bowl with lemon leaves and arrange the lemons on top.

Ideas for Party Favors

sparkling splits

Wrap splits of sparkling wine in festive tissue paper, leaving the neck and foil exposed. Use raffia to tie the paper in place and to attach a decorative gift tag with the recipient's name or a festive message. Put each bottle in a silver or gold take-out carton (available at party-supply and craft stores).

sweet wishes

Slip a few fortune cookies into small mesh gift bags or small cellophane bags from a party-supply store. You can add homemade cookies or wrapped candies as well. Place a raffle ticket (also sold at party-supply stores) or a handwritten message in each bag. Tie the bags with a piece of natural twine or a silver or gold ribbon.

Ideas for Lighting Up New Year's

votive place cards

Arrange laurel or sage leaves on plates at each place setting to form a star pattern. Set a tea light in a pretty votive holder on top of the leaves and attach a tag with a guest's name written on it in colored ink. Place more matching candles around the room.

candle cubes

For a fresh, modern look, place dripless cube-shaped candles on wooden coasters with a contemporary design. Set the candles in the center of the table in a rectangular cluster. You can pick up the look elsewhere in the space with larger square or rectangular candles of varying sizes and heights.

shiny votives

Buy several small, colored glass votive holders and put a cream-hued votive in each. Tie raffia, jute twine, or ribbon around the top of each holder. Line the candles up in two or more rows, running down the center of the table, along the mantel, or on the buffet.

Drinks

Mojito Peppermint Fizz **70**

Ginger Cosmopolitan **70**

French 75 Champagne Cocktail **73**

Grapefruit Champagne Punch **73**

Hot Rum Coffee **74**

Hot Mulled Cider **74**

Winter Swizzle **77**

Clementine-Mint Sparkler **77**

Pomegranate Frost **78**

Apple-Ginger Fizz **78**

81 Chapel Hill Cocktail

81 Cranberry-Lime Punch

82 Lemon Verbena Drop with Thyme

82 Ruby Red Grapefruit Martini

85 Camparini

85 Lillet Cocktail

86 Apple Cider Cocktail

86 Boston Eggnog with Cardamom

88 Serving Wine for the Holidays

Mojito Peppermint Fizz

serves 2

Ice cubes

½ cup (4 fl oz/125 ml) white rum

¼ cup (2 fl oz/60 ml) fresh lime juice

2 tablespoons peppermint liqueur

2 tablespoons superfine (caster) sugar

16 fresh mint leaves, finely shredded, plus 2 small sprigs for garnish

2 long candy canes for garnish

Select 2 highball glasses. Fill a tall cocktail shaker three-fourths full with ice. Add the rum, lime juice, peppermint liqueur, sugar, and shredded mint. Cover with the lid and shake vigorously for 10 seconds. Open the shaker and evenly divide the liquid and ice between the glasses. Garnish each glass with a mint sprig and a candy cane and serve at once.

Ginger Cosmopolitan

serves 2

2 round slices peeled fresh ginger, each about ⅛ inch (3 mm) thick, plus 12–14 round, paper-thin slices of peeled fresh ginger for garnish

2 tablespoons fresh lime juice

Ice cubes

½ cup (4 fl oz/125 ml) cranberry juice

⅓ cup (3 fl oz/80 ml) vodka

2 tablespoons Cointreau

Chill 2 martini glasses. Drop the 2 thicker slices of the ginger into the bottom of a tall cocktail shaker and add the lime juice. Using a muddler or the end of a wooden spoon, crush the ginger until almost pulverized. Fill the shaker half full with ice and add the cranberry juice, vodka, and Cointreau. Cover with the lid and shake vigorously for 10 seconds, then strain through the ice strainer and a fine-mesh sieve into the chilled glasses. Garnish each glass with 6 or 7 ginger slices threaded onto a cocktail pick. Serve at once.

French 75 Champagne Cocktail

serves 4

1 bottle (24 fl oz/750 ml) Champagne

Ice cubes

1 cup (8 fl oz/250 ml) gin

½ cup (4 fl oz/125 ml) fresh lemon juice

2 ½ tablespoons superfine
(caster) sugar

4 lemon peel strips, each about ¼ inch
(6 mm) wide and 3–4 inches
(7.5–10 cm) long

Chill the Champagne and 4 Champagne flutes or stemmed glasses. Fill a tall cocktail shaker half full with ice. Add the gin, lemon juice, and sugar. Cover with the lid and shake vigorously for 10 seconds. Strain into the chilled glasses. Top with a splash of Champagne. Float a lemon strip on top of each drink and serve at once.

Grapefruit Champagne Punch

serves 12

1 bottle (24 fl oz/750 ml) Champagne

4 cups (32 fl oz/1 l) fresh grapefruit juice

2 cups (16 fl oz/500 ml) fresh
orange juice

1 cup *each* (8 fl oz/250 ml) fresh
lemon juice and fresh lime juice

1 cup (7 oz/220 g) superfine
(caster) sugar

4 teaspoons crème de cassis

12 orange peel strips, each about ¼ inch
(6 mm) wide and 3–4 inches
(7.5–10 cm) long

Chill the Champagne. In a pitcher, combine the grapefruit, orange, lemon, and lime juices. Add the sugar and stir to dissolve completely. Refrigerate the pitcher until the juices are well chilled.

Select 12 Champagne flutes or stemmed glasses. Remove the Champagne and pitcher from the refrigerator. Add the Champagne to the pitcher and stir gently. Pour the punch into the glasses. Add 1 teaspoon crème de cassis to each glass. It will sink to the bottom of the glass. Garnish each glass with an orange strip and serve at once.

Hot Rum Coffee

serves 4

2 cups (16 fl oz/500 ml) hot coffee

½ cup (4 fl oz/125 ml)
half-and-half (half cream), heated

2 ½ tablespoons sugar

⅛ teaspoon *each* ground cardamom
and freshly grated nutmeg

¾ cup (6 fl oz/180 ml) amber rum

Grated chocolate for garnish

Select 4 mugs. In a pitcher, stir together the coffee, half-and-half, sugar, cardamom, and nutmeg. Pour 3 tablespoons of the rum into each mug, and top with the warm coffee mixture. Stir gently, sprinkle the top with the chocolate, and serve at once.

Hot Mulled Cider

serves 6

4 cups (32 fl oz/1 l) apple cider

4 teaspoons honey

½ teaspoon ground allspice

½ teaspoon freshly grated nutmeg

8 cloves

8 cinnamon sticks

1 cup plus 2 tablespoons
(9 fl oz/280 ml) brandy

Select 6 mugs or glasses. In a saucepan over medium heat, combine the cider, honey, allspice, nutmeg, cloves, and 2 of the cinnamon sticks. Bring to just below a simmer and reduce the heat to low. Cook for about 20 minutes.

Pour 3 tablespoons of the brandy into each mug. Divide the hot cider mixture evenly among the mugs, pouring it through a fine-mesh sieve. Garnish each serving with a cinnamon stick and serve at once.

Winter Swizzle

serves 2

Ice cubes

1 cup (8 fl oz/250 ml) fresh
grapefruit juice

1 teaspoon honey

2 pinches of ground cardamom

2 pinches of ground cinnamon

1 bottle (12 fl oz/375 ml) ginger ale

Candied grapefruit peel
(page 266) for garnish (optional)

Chill 2 martini glasses. Fill a tall cocktail shaker half full with ice. Add the grapefruit juice, honey, cardamom, and cinnamon. Cover with the lid and shake vigorously for 10 seconds. Strain into the chilled glasses. Top with a splash of ginger ale and garnish with a slice of candied grapefuit peel cut into a diamond or other shape, if desired. Serve at once.

Clementine-Mint Sparkler

serves 2

Ice cubes

12 mint leaves, finely shredded,
plus 2 whole leaves for garnish

¼ cup (2 fl oz/60 ml) fresh lemon juice

1 cup (8 fl oz/250 ml) fresh clementine
mandarin juice

1 bottle (24 fl oz/750 ml)
sparkling water

Clementine mandarin tops
or slices for garnish

Fill 2 highball or other tall glasses with ice. Divide the shredded mint between the glasses. Pour half of the lemon juice and half of the clementine juice into each glass. Top with sparkling water and stir well. Garnish each glass with a clementine top and a whole mint leaf and serve at once.

Pomegranate Frost

serves 6

Ice cubes or pomegranate ice cubes
(see serving tip on page 81)

1 ½ cups (12 fl oz/375 ml)
pomegranate juice

1 ½ cups (12 fl oz/375 ml)
cranberry juice

½ cup *each* (4 fl oz/125 ml) fresh Meyer
lemon juice and fresh lime juice

1 bottle (24 fl oz/750 ml)
sparkling water

8 fresh mint leaves, finely shredded

Fill a pitcher half full with ice. Add the pomegranate juice, cranberry juice, lemon juice, lime juice, 1 ½ cups (12 fl oz/375 ml) of the sparkling water, and the shredded mint and stir until well mixed.

Fill 6 tall glasses with ice. Pour the mixture into the glasses and serve at once.

Apple-Ginger Fizz

serves 4

Ice cubes

1 ½ cups (12 fl oz/375 ml) apple cider

½ cup (4 fl oz/125 ml) fresh lime juice

1 bottle (12 fl oz/375 ml) ginger beer

4 lime wedges for serving

Fill 4 highball or tall glasses with ice. Fill a tall cocktail shaker half full with ice. Add the apple cider and lime juice. Cover with the lid and shake vigorously for 20 seconds. Strain into the glasses, filling them no more than three-fourths full. Top each drink with ¼ cup (2 fl oz/60 ml) of the ginger beer, garnish with a lime wedge, and serve at once.

Chapel Hill Cocktail

serves 4

Ice cubes

1 cup (8 fl oz/250 ml) bourbon

1 cup (8 fl oz/250 ml) triple sec

¼ cup (2 fl oz/60 ml) fresh lemon juice, preferably Meyer

4 orange peel strips for garnish

Chill 4 martini glasses. Fill a tall cocktail shaker half full with ice. Add the bourbon, triple sec, and lemon juice. Cover with the lid and shake vigorously for 10 seconds. Strain into the chilled glasses. Garnish each glass with an orange peel strip and serve at once.

Cranberry-Lime Punch

serves 12

1 tablespoon honey

4 cups (32 fl oz/1 l) cranberry juice

¾ cup (6 fl oz/180 ml) fresh lime juice

One can (12 fl oz/375 ml) lemon soda

Ice cubes

Grated zest of 4–6 limes

serving tip

To make colorful and flavorful ice cubes, place some freshly grated citrus zest, shredded fresh mint, or pomegranate seeds in each compartment of an ice-cube tray, fill with water, and freeze until solid.

Select 12 tumblers or old-fashioned glasses. In a small bowl, stir together the honey and a little warm water to dissolve the honey. In a punch bowl or pitcher, combine the cranberry juice, lime juice, and honey mixture and stir until well blended. Add the lemon soda and stir gently. Fill the tumblers half full with ice. Ladle or pour the punch into the glasses and garnish each glass with the lime zest. Serve at once.

Lemon Verbena Drop with Thyme

serves 2

2 cups (16 oz/500 g) sugar
for the sugar garnish (optional),
plus 3 tablespoons

⅓ cup (3 fl oz/80 ml) water

8 sprigs fresh thyme

¼ cup *each* (2 fl oz/60 ml) vodka and
lemon verbena–infused vodka

¼ cup (2 fl oz/60 ml) fresh lemon juice

Ice cubes

prep tip

To make infused vodka, wash 5 fresh
lemon verbena sprigs, pat dry, and place
in a jar with 2 cups (16 fl oz/500 ml)
vodka for 12–24 hours.

To make the optional sugar garnish, have ready a bowl of ice water. Lightly oil a baking sheet. In a heavy saucepan over medium heat, stir the 2 cups sugar with a wooden spoon until the sugar melts and turns a golden caramel color, about 5 minutes. Remove from the heat and plunge the bottom of the pan into the ice water for exactly 10 seconds to halt the cooking. Immediately spoon the hot caramel out onto the prepared baking sheet, creating small strands. Let cool until hard, and then crack into tiny shards. Set aside.

To make a sugar syrup, in a saucepan over medium-high heat, bring the water to a simmer. Add the 3 tablespoons sugar and stir until completely dissolved. Remove from the heat and let cool to room temperature.

Chill 2 martini glasses. In a tall cocktail shaker, combine the thyme sprigs with the sugar syrup. Using a muddler or the handle of a wooden spoon, lightly crush and pound the thyme for 1 minute. Add the vodka, the infused vodka, and the lemon juice. Fill the shaker half full with ice, cover with the lid, and shake vigorously for 10 seconds. Strain into the chilled glasses. Balance a few sugar shards on each rim. (The remaining shards can be stored, if using, in an airtight container at room temperature for up to 3 days). Serve at once.

Ruby Red Grapefruit Martini

serves 2

Ice cubes

½ cup (4 fl oz/125 ml) fresh Ruby Red
grapefruit juice

½ cup (4 fl oz/125 ml) vodka

4 dashes of orange bitters

2 orange or grapefruit peel strips

Chill 2 martini glasses. Fill a tall cocktail shaker half full with ice. Add the grapefruit juice, vodka, and bitters. Cover with the lid and shake vigorously for 10 seconds. Strain into the chilled glasses. Garnish each glass with a curled orange or grapefruit strip and serve at once.

Camparini

serves 2

Ice cubes

½ cup (4 fl oz/125 ml) Campari

½ cup (4 fl oz/125 ml) fresh
grapefruit juice

½ cup (4 fl oz/125 ml) sweet vermouth

1 bottle (24 fl oz/750 ml)
sparkling water

2 lemon twists for garnish

Select 2 highball glasses. Fill a tall cocktail shaker half full with ice. Add the Campari, grapefruit juice, and vermouth. Cover with the lid and shake vigorously for 10 seconds. Strain into the glasses. Top with a splash of sparkling water. Garnish each glass with a lemon twist and serve at once.

Lillet Cocktail

serves 2

Ice cubes

⅓ cup (3 fl oz/80 ml) Lillet Blanc

⅓ cup (3 fl oz/80 ml) gin

2 tablespoons fresh lemon juice

2 dashes of orange bitters

1 bottle (24 fl oz/750 ml)
sparkling water

2 lemon peel strips, curled
loosely, for garnish

Select 2 small glasses. Fill a tall cocktail shaker half full with ice. Add the Lillet Blanc, gin, lemon juice, and bitters. Cover with the lid and shake vigorously for 10 seconds. Strain into the glasses. Top with a splash of sparkling water. Garnish each glass with a curled lemon strip and serve at once.

Apple Cider Cocktail

serves 2

Ice cubes

½ cup (4 fl oz/125 ml) apple cider

¼ cup (2 fl oz/60 ml) Calvados

¼ cup (2 fl oz/60 ml) brandy

¼ cup (2 fl oz/60 ml) fresh lemon juice

2 teaspoons pure maple syrup

2 apple slices, cut sides rubbed with lemon juice, for garnish

Chill 2 cocktail glasses. Fill a tall cocktail shaker half full with ice. Add the apple cider, Calvados, brandy, lemon juice, and maple syrup. Cover with the lid and shake vigorously for 10 seconds. Strain into the chilled glasses. For the fruit garnish, cut a thin slit partway into each apple slice and perch a slice on the rim of each glass. Serve at once.

Boston Eggnog with Cardamom

serves 2

Ice cubes

¾ cup (6 fl oz/180 ml) whole milk

¼ cup (2 fl oz/60 ml) *each* brandy, amber rum, and Madeira

2 large egg yolks, lightly beaten

2 tablespoons sugar

2 or 3 dashes of ground cardamom, plus extra for garnish

2 or 3 pinches of freshly grated nutmeg

2 cinnamon sticks for garnish

Select 2 old-fashioned glasses or mugs. Fill a tall cocktail shaker half full with ice. Add the milk, brandy, rum, Madeira, egg yolks, sugar, cardamom, and nutmeg. Cover with the lid and shake vigorously for 10 seconds. Strain into the glasses. Garnish each glass with a cinnamon stick and a sprinkle of cardamom, and serve at once.

Note: This recipe calls for raw egg yolks. While the incidence of bacteria in raw eggs is rare, anyone with a compromised immune system should use caution.

Serving Wine for the Holidays

Pouring good wines, chosen to bring out the best in the foods they accompany, will enhance the pleasure of any holiday party, dressy or casual. And good wine doesn't have to mean fancy labels or big price tags.

selecting and chilling wines

For big holiday gatherings, such as cocktail parties and open houses, you'll want to offer a white, a red, and perhaps a sparkling wine (especially for New Year's Eve parties).

A few weeks before the season begins, drop by a trusted wine store with your holiday menus in hand and ask for pairing recommendations. Have a per-bottle budget range in mind, and remember that buying cases can often save you money. Any unused bottles will help build your cellar for the coming year.

Chill white and sparkling wines for at least 2 hours in the refrigerator or for 20 minutes in an ice bucket filled with equal parts ice and water. Sparkling wines should be served very cold (42°–45°F/6°–7°C), whites cold (50°F/10°C), and reds at cool room temperature.

pouring and presenting wines

Pour predinner wine (or wine served at an open house or cocktail party) as soon as guests arrive. For dinner parties, wait until the guests are seated before pouring the wine. Fill wineglasses to the widest part of the glass, or three-fourths full, so there's room at the top for the bouquet to develop.

When serving chilled bottles, wrap them in a cloth napkin to insulate them and to prevent drips. You can use decanters to serve any wine, but they are a good idea for older wines, which may contain sediment, and for young or highly tannic wines, which can benefit from the aeration that occurs as you pour them from the bottle. Decanters also add an elegant touch to any table.

matching food & wine

Pairing food and wine is less about rules like "red with meat, white with fish" and more about matching the characteristics of a dish (light, rich, sweet, acidic, creamy) with a wine that reflects the same qualities.

HORS D'OEUVRES

pair holiday nibbles with a sparkling wine, a fruity white, a rosé, or a light red

sparkling Champagne, Prosecco, *cava*

white Gewürztraminer, Grüner Veltliner, Riesling, Sauvignon Blanc

red Beaujolais, Lambrusco, Pinot Noir

SPICY DISHES

serve a low-alcohol, fruity white or a light, spicy red

white Moscato d'Asti, Pinot Grigio, Pinot Gris, Riesling, Soave, Verdicchio

red Beaujolais, Brunello, Pinot Noir, Primitivo, Nebbiolo, Zinfandel

HEAVY SAUCES

pair with a heavy, full-bodied white or a big, assertive red

white California Chardonnay, Sauvignon Blanc, Viognier

red Cabernet Sauvignon, Châteauneuf-du-Pape, Merlot, Syrah, Zinfandel

PASTA

serve lighter pastas with a dry white, and tomato-based or heartier pastas with a full-bodied, spicy red

white Friulano, Pinot Grigio, Soave, Viognier, white Burgundy

red Cabernet Sauvignon, Chianti, Sangiovese, Syrah, Valpolicella

SEAFOOD

choose a light or full-bodied white, a dry rosé, or a light red with salmon and meatier fish; or a sparkling or mineraly white with shellfish

white Chardonnay, Muscadet, Pinot Gris, Riesling, Sauvignon Blanc, Viognier

reds Beaujolais, light Côtes du Rhône, Pinot Noir

ACIDIC DISHES

with tomato or citrus, pair a high-acid white or red

white Pouilly-Fumé, Sancerre, Sauvignon Blanc, Sémillon, white Bordeaux

red Chianti, Dolcetto, Zinfandel

ROASTED MEATS

serve with a robust, full-bodied, or spicy red

red Barolo, Bordeaux, Cabernet Sauvignon, or a big Super Tuscan

POULTRY

serve with a crisp, dry white or a spicy, medium-bodied red

white Chardonnay, medium-dry Gewürztraminer, Sauvignon Blanc

red Beaujolais, Grenache, Malbec, Pinot Noir, Syrah, Tempranillo

HAM

offer a slightly sweet white or a medium-bodied, spicy red

white Gewürztraminer, Pinot Gris, Riesling

red Pinot Noir, Syrah, Zinfandel

CHEESE

pair with sparkling wine; a big, luscious white; a fruity red; or a sweet dessert wine

sparkling Champagne, Prosecco, *cava*

white Sauvignon Blanc, Sancerre

red Pinot Noir, Tempranillo, Zinfandel

dessert Madeira, Muscat, port, Sauternes

DESSERTS

choose a sweet dessert white or a fortified red

white Eiswein, muscat, Sauternes, *vin santo*

red Banyuls, Madeira, port, sherry

Hors d'Oeuvres

Serving Oysters 92

Cheese Straws with Sesame Seeds 94

Crunchy Sweet Potato Chips 97

Caramelized Onion and Sour Cream Dip 97

Cheddar and Roasted Red Pepper Dip 98

Three-Spice Chex-and-Nut Mix 98

Dates Stuffed with Fontina and Hazelnuts 99

Endive with Gorgonzola, Pear, and Walnuts 100

Ricotta-Stuffed Cherry Tomatoes 100

Artisanal-Cheese Fondue 102

103 Warm Citrus Olives

103 Baked Goat Cheese with Honey and Apples

104 Serving an Antipasto Platter

107 Sautéed Scallops with Meyer Lemon Relish

108 Cucumbers with Pickled Ginger and Crab

111 Smoked Salmon Canapés with Caviar

112 Beef Crostini with Horseradish and Watercress

113 Grilled Lamb Chops with Olive-Mint Tapenade

114 Assorted Panini Bites

117 Filet Mignon Skewers with Balsamic Reduction

sherry mignonette

MAKES ABOUT ⅓ CUP (3 FL OZ/80 ML)

3 tablespoons fresh lemon juice

2 tablespoons sherry vinegar

1 small shallot, minced

1 teaspoon coarsely ground pepper

¼ teaspoon salt

In a bowl, stir together the lemon juice and vinegar. Add in the shallot, pepper, and salt and stir until well blended. Cover tightly and refrigerate until ready to serve. The sauce can be prepared up to 1 day in advance.

ginger mignonette

MAKES ABOUT ⅔ CUP (5 FL OZ/160 ML)

⅔ cup (5 fl oz/160 ml) white wine vinegar

1 ½ teaspoons peeled and minced fresh ginger

1 green (spring) onion, including tender green tops, thinly sliced

1 ½ teaspoons grated lemon zest

1 teaspoon coarsely ground pepper

¼ teaspoon salt

In a bowl, stir together the vinegar, ginger, green onion, and lemon zest. Stir in the pepper and salt. Cover tightly and refrigerate until ready to serve. The sauce can be prepared up to 1 day in advance.

Serving Oysters

For holiday entertaining, few appetizers have the visual impact and luxurious allure of a raw bar with freshly shucked oysters on the half shell. And because there's no cooking involved, setting one up is remarkably easy.

selecting oysters

Order oysters well in advance of your party from a good fishmonger or grocery store. Plan on 6 to 12 oysters per guest. Unless you have experience shucking oysters, order them shucked and on ice. They should be live until just before they're eaten, so arrange for pickup or delivery no more than a few hours before your party. Ask your fishmonger to include some seaweed for decorating, as well as extra crushed ice.

regional favorites

You can buy oysters of a single type, or choose two or three varieties with different characteristics. Ask your fishmonger for recommendations. Popular Atlantic varieties include large, briny Bluepoints and sweet, delicate Malpeques from Prince Edward Island. Pacific varieties range from tiny, yet flavorful Olympias and plump, buttery Kumamotos to mild, creamy Miyagis and large, rich Hog Island Sweetwaters.

setting up a raw bar

Just before the party, cover a large platter or serving tray with crushed ice. Shuck enough oysters to cover the surface of the platter. You can also add other freshly shucked shellfish, such as clams, or you can surround the arrangement with cooked and peeled shrimp (prawns). Decorate the platter with lemon wedges and, if you like, a few strands of seaweed. Serve a mignonette (see left), hot sauce, lemon wedges, cracked black pepper, and slices of sweet or sourdough baguette on the side. Pour a sparkling wine, a dry white such as a Sauvignon Blanc, or a citrusy Muscadet with the oysters.

Cheese straws are a fun, easy-to-eat, and impressive alternative to cheese and crackers. Poppy seeds can be used in place of the sesame seeds. The straws can be made ahead but are especially good served still warm from the oven.

Cheese Straws with Sesame Seeds

serves 12–14

½ lb (250 g) sharp Cheddar cheese, shredded

2 oz (60 g) Parmesan cheese, grated

½ cup (4 oz/125 g) unsalted butter, at room temperature

½ teaspoon freshly ground white pepper

¼ teaspoon cayenne pepper

1 cup (5 oz/ 155 g) all-purpose (plain) flour

½ cup (2 oz/60 g) black or white sesame seeds

serving tip

For a creative presentation, stand the cheese straws in decorative glasses or vases and place near a cocktail area so guests can serve themselves.

In a food processor, combine the cheeses, butter, white pepper, and cayenne pepper and process to a smooth paste. Slowly add the flour, pulsing to blend. When all of the flour is incorporated, gather the dough into a ball. Wrap in plastic wrap and refrigerate for at least 1 hour and up to 3 hours.

Preheat the oven to 350°F (180°C). Lightly grease a baking sheet with butter or line it with parchment (baking) paper.

Remove the chilled dough from the refrigerator and cut it into 6 equal pieces. On a lightly floured work surface, use your palm to roll each piece into a rope about the diameter of a drinking straw. Cut each rope into 6–8-inch (15–20-cm) lengths, or shorter if you like. Sprinkle the sesame seeds evenly on a sheet of aluminum foil. Roll each straw in the seeds, coating lightly on all sides. Place the straws about 1 inch (2.5 cm) apart on the prepared baking sheet.

Bake until golden brown and lightly crisp, 15–20 minutes. Transfer the baking sheet to a wire rack and let cool for 5–10 minutes. (Or, let cool completely and store the straws in an airtight container for up to 8 hours.) Transfer the cheese straws to a platter and serve warm.

Crunchy Sweet Potato Chips

serves 6

2 large sweet potatoes

Canola oil for deep-frying

Sea salt

serving tip

Serve the chips on their own or with a dip such as the Cheddar and Roasted Red Pepper Dip (page 98).

Peel the sweet potatoes. Using a mandoline or a large, sharp chef's knife, cut the potatoes into slices about ⅛ inch (3 cm) thick. Put the slices in a bowl of ice water and refrigerate for at least 1 hour and up to 8 hours.

Drain and dry the potato slices thoroughly. Pour oil to a depth of 1½–2 inches (4–5 cm) in a large frying pan and place over medium-high heat. When the oil is hot, add the potato slices a few at a time; do not crowd the pan. Fry, turning once, until crisp and golden, about 2 minutes total. Using tongs or a slotted spoon, transfer to paper towels to drain. Repeat until all the chips are fried. Sprinkle with the sea salt and serve warm or at room temperature.

Caramelized Onion and Sour Cream Dip

serves 8

1 lb (500 g) yellow onions

3 tablespoons unsalted butter

3 tablespoons extra-virgin olive oil

1 teaspoon salt

1 teaspoon freshly ground pepper

2 cups (1 lb/500 g) low-fat sour cream

2 teaspoons minced fresh thyme

1 teaspoon white balsamic vinegar

Using a mandoline or a large, sharp chef's knife, cut the onions into slices about ⅛ inch (3 mm) thick. Cut the slices in half.

In a saucepan over medium heat, melt the butter with the olive oil. Add the onions and sprinkle with the salt and pepper. Stir, then reduce the heat to low and cook, uncovered, stirring occasionally, until the onions are deep golden brown, about 20 minutes. Let cool to room temperature. (The onions can be cooked up to 2 days ahead, covered, and refrigerated.)

When the onions are cool, transfer to a blender or food processor. Add 1 cup (8 oz/250 g) of the sour cream, the thyme, and the vinegar and process to a coarse purée. Transfer to a bowl and stir in the remaining 1 cup sour cream. (The dip can be covered and refrigerated for up to 8 hours before serving.)

Transfer to a serving bowl and serve at room temperature.

Cheddar and Roasted Red Pepper Dip

serves 8–10

2 ½ cups (10 oz/315 g) shredded
Cheddar cheese

¾ cup (4 ½ oz/135 g) roasted red
peppers packed in olive-oil, drained
and coarsely chopped

¼ cup (2 oz/60 g) low-fat sour cream

2 tablespoons heavy (double) cream

2 tablespoons minced shallots

½ teaspoon salt

½ teaspoon freshly ground
white pepper

In a blender or food processor, combine the cheese, roasted peppers, sour cream, heavy cream, and shallots and process until smooth, about 1 minute. Add the salt and pepper and pulse a few times just to blend. Taste and adjust the seasoning. (The dip can be covered and refrigerated for up to 2 days before serving.) Transfer to a serving bowl and serve at room temperature.

Three-Spice Chex-and-Nut Mix

serves 6–8

2 cups (6 oz/185 g) *each* Rice Chex,
Wheat Chex, Corn Chex, and Cheerios

½ cup (2 ½ oz/75 g) roasted peanuts

½ cup (2 oz/60 g) roasted pistachios

3 tablespoons unsalted butter

¼ teaspoon fennel seeds, coarsely
crushed in a mortar or spice grinder

¼ teaspoon *each* chili powder
and ground cumin

¼ teaspoon sea salt

Preheat the oven to 200°F (95°C). Combine the cereals and nuts in a roasting pan or rimmed baking sheet. Set aside.

In a small saucepan over low heat, melt the butter and heat until it starts to color, about 2 minutes. Remove from the heat and stir in the fennel seeds, chili powder, cumin, and salt. Pour the mixture over the cereal and nuts and stir until well blended.

Bake, stirring every 20–30 minutes, until crispy, about 2 hours. Remove from the oven, let cool slightly, and serve warm, or serve at room temperature. (The mix can be made up to 1 week in advance and stored in an airtight container at room temperature.)

These appetizers carry the complementary tastes and textures of cheese, fruit, and nuts in a single bite. They can be made up to 24 hours in advance and refrigerated for easy party prep. Bring to room temperature before serving.

Dates Stuffed with Fontina and Hazelnuts

serves 6–8

18 dates, preferably Medjool

⅓ cup (1 ½ oz/45 g) hazelnuts (filberts)

¼ lb (125 g) fontina cheese, finely diced

shopping tip

Other combinations of cheese and nuts can be used, such as Parmesan slivers and almonds, or thinly sliced pecorino and walnuts.

Make a slit in each date and gently remove the pit. Set the dates aside.

Place the hazelnuts in a frying pan over medium heat. Toast, stirring often, until the nuts are fragrant and the skins start to wrinkle, 10–15 minutes. Transfer to a plate and let cool slightly. When the nuts are cool enough to handle but still warm, wrap in a kitchen towel and rub vigorously to remove the skins. Coarsely chop the nuts.

Combine the cheese and hazelnuts in a bowl and, using your fingertips, toss to mix well. Stuff the cavity of each date with about 1 teaspoon of the cheese-nut mixture. Arrange on a platter and serve.

These colorful and savory treats, pairing vegetables and cheese, are easy to make. Serve them on a platter at a cocktail party or as an appetizer before dinner. You can substitute any creamy cheese or crème fraîche for the Gorgonzola and ricotta.

Endive with Gorgonzola, Pear, and Walnuts

serves 8

½ cup (2 oz/60 g) walnuts

2 heads Belgian endive (chicory/witloof)

4 firm but ripe pears such as Bosc

6 oz (185 g) Gorgonzola cheese, at room temperature

Frisèe leaves for garnish

Preheat the oven to 350°F (180°C). Place the walnuts in a single layer on a baking sheet and bake, stirring once or twice, until fragrant and lightly toasted, 10–12 minutes. Pour onto a plate and let cool, then chop coarsely.

Separate the leaves of the endives. Choose about 40 of the pale ivory to light green inner leaves (reserve the others for another use).

Halve and core the pears, then finely chop. Spread a teaspoonful of the cheese on the base of each endive leaf. Top with a little pear, a sprinkle of nuts, and a few frisèe leaves. Serve at once.

Ricotta-Stuffed Cherry Tomatoes

serves 8

24 cherry tomatoes

¾ cup (6 oz/185 g) low-fat ricotta cheese, drained in a sieve for 1 hour

2 tablespoons minced fresh flat-leaf (Italian) parsley

1–2 tablespoons heavy (double) cream, if needed

Preheat the oven to 400°F (200°C).

Cut a slice off the top of each cherry tomato and set the tops aside. Carefully scoop out and discard the seeds and pulp.

In a bowl, combine the ricotta and parsley and mash together with a fork to make a paste, adding the cream if needed to soften.

Fill each cherry tomato with a little of the cheese mixture. Replace the tomato tops. Place the stuffed tomatoes on a baking sheet. Roast until the cheese is warm throughout and the tomatoes are shiny and soft but not collapsing, 10–12 minutes. Transfer to a platter and serve warm.

Artisanal cheeses are made in smaller quantities using traditional cheese-making methods and aging techniques to create products with nuanced flavor and superior texture. Pair the fondue with a green salad for a casual winter supper.

Artisanal-Cheese Fondue

serves 8

6 cloves garlic

1 bottle (24 fl oz/750 ml) Sauvignon Blanc or other dry white wine

½ teaspoon salt

5 oz (155 g) mild blue cheese such as Point Reyes blue, crumbled

½ lb (250 g) nutty, semifirm cheese such as Gruyère, shredded or cut into cubes

½ lb (250 g) sharp, firm cheese such as Vella Dry Jack, grated, chopped, or cut into shavings with a vegetable peeler

1 tablespoon unsalted butter

½ teaspoon freshly ground pepper

¼ teaspoon freshly grated nutmeg

1 ½ day-old baguettes, cut into 1-inch (2.5-cm) cubes

Preheat the oven to 250°F (120°C). Place a ceramic fondue pot in the oven.

Using a garlic press, squeeze the garlic cloves into a heavy saucepan. Place the pan over medium-high heat and add the wine and salt. Heat just until bubbles begin to appear around the edges of the pot.

Add all of the cheeses to the hot wine mixture. Using a wooden spoon, stir until the cheeses are nearly melted, about 10 minutes. Reduce the heat to medium-low; add the butter, pepper, and nutmeg; and stir until the cheese is completely melted and the mixture is smooth, 1–2 minutes longer.

To serve, remove the fondue pot from the oven. Light the fondue burner and place it on the dining table, kitchen counter, or sideboard. Pour the cheese mixture into the warmed fondue pot and place over the burner. Serve with the bread cubes alongside. Let diners help themselves to the bread cubes, instructing them to spear a cube through the crust side to help anchor it to the fork, and then swirl the bread in the fondue.

Warm Citrus Olives

serves 6

1 cup (5 oz/155 g) Niçoise, Kalamata, or picholine olives

¼ cup (2 fl oz/60 ml) extra-virgin olive oil

2 large cloves garlic, sliced

½ teaspoon fennel seeds, coarsely crushed in a mortar or spice grinder

1 tablespoon fresh lemon juice

Rinse the olives well and pat dry thoroughly.

In a frying pan over medium heat, warm the olive oil. Add the garlic and heat until it starts to color, about 1 minute. Stir in the olives and fennel seeds and cook until the olives are hot throughout, about 2 minutes. Remove from the heat and let cool. Stir the lemon juice into the olives and transfer to a tightly covered container. Let stand for at least 8 hours and up to 24 hours at room temperature, shaking occasionally to redistribute the seasoning.

To serve, preheat the oven to 350°F (180°C). Put the olives and their marinade in a baking dish and bake until they are warm throughout, about 10 minutes.

Using a slotted spoon, lift the olives out of the marinade and transfer to a serving dish. Serve warm, not hot, with an empty bowl alongside for pits.

Baked Goat Cheese with Honey and Apples

serves 8–10

½-lb (250-g) log soft fresh goat cheese

2 crisp apples such as Granny Smith or Gala

3 tablespoons honey

1 teaspoon fresh lemon juice

Toasted thin baguette slices or crackers for serving

Preheat the oven to 400°F (200°C).

Place the log of goat cheese on a rimmed baking sheet. Halve and core the apples and thinly slice them lengthwise. Put the apples in a bowl, add 1 tablespoon of the honey and the lemon juice, and turn the apples to coat. Drizzle the remaining 2 tablespoons honey over the cheese, and layer the apple slices on top.

Bake until the cheese is warm throughout and softened and the apples are tender, 8–10 minutes. Using a wide spatula, transfer the cheese log to a platter. Serve warm with the baguette slices.

Warm Citrus Olives (page 103)

Marinated roasted red peppers

Prosciutto-wrapped melon, figs, or pears

Assorted cured meats such as salami, mortadella, and *bresaola*

Aged pecorino cheese

serve with *bread sticks, herbed crackers; Prosecco, Campari and soda*

pinzimonio

Fresh vegetables such as fennel, celery hearts, carrots, bell peppers (capsicums)

Olive oil, sea salt, and pepper

Bite-sized mozzarella balls skewered with cherry tomatoes and fresh basil

Parmesan chunks drizzled with balsamic vinegar

serve with *focaccia, baguette rounds; sparkling wine, French Chardonnay*

mediterranean

Marinated artichokes

Toasted Marcona almonds with sea salt

Bread sticks wrapped with *serrano* ham

Crostini with tapenade

Crostini with goat cheese and chutney

serve with *olive bread, grape focaccia; Albariño, cava, rosé, sherry*

Serving an Antipasto Platter

A platter of Mediterranean-style savory bites partners well with predinner drinks at holiday gatherings. It is an easy option for cocktail parties, open houses, and lunch buffets, too, because most of the items are store-bought.

the elements

Start with a visit to a good deli or specialty-foods store to find ready-made items like olives; specialty nuts, such as Marcona almonds; artisanal cheeses, such as pecorino, Manchego, mozzarella, and fresh goat cheese; spreads, such as tapenade; and cured meats, including prosciutto, salami, mortadella, and *coppa*. Serve four to six items, and plan on 1 to 2 ounces (30 to 60 g) of each per guest. You can supplement these offerings with raw or roasted vegetables with a Mediterranean-style dipping sauce.

assembly

Choose an attractive tray, platter, or cutting board. Or, create a dramatic presentation using a long, narrow platter, a tiered charcuterie "tower," or several matching small plates, with a single antipasto on each. Arrange the food to create an unfussy, natural look, piling items casually and rolling or loosely folding sliced meats. Decorate with grape leaves, fresh herbs such as sage, rosemary, or thyme. Place small plates, decorative cocktail picks or salad forks, and cocktail napkins next to the antipasto assortment.

accompaniments

Serve a basket of thinly sliced baguette rounds, slices of coarse country bread, cubes of focaccia, or crackers. You can also set out bread sticks or cheese straws (page 94) in tall glasses. Sparkling wines such as Prosecco, *cava*, Champagne, and California sparkling wine are a perfect match for the salty, oily flavors of antipasti, as are whites such as Vernaccia, Soave, and Falanghina and light reds, including Lambrusco and Pinot Noir. Ice-cold beer and Italian aperitifs, such as Campari, are also good choices.

Sautéed Scallops with Meyer Lemon Relish

serves 8

RELISH

2 Meyer lemons, quartered and seeded

1 shallot, coarsely chopped

2 tablespoons fresh flat-leaf (Italian) parsley leaves

1 teaspoon *each* sugar and coriander seeds

1 teaspoon white balsamic vinegar

Salt and freshly ground white pepper

VINAIGRETTE

1 cup (8 fl oz/250 ml) fresh Meyer lemon juice

3 tablespoons fresh lime juice

1 tablespoon minced shallot

1 tablespoon canola oil

Salt and freshly ground white pepper

16 sea scallops

1 tablespoon canola oil

¼ cup (2 fl oz/60 ml) dry white wine

2 tablespoons chicken stock

1 teaspoon white balsamic vinegar

1 teaspoon *each* salt and freshly ground white pepper

4 cups (4 oz/125 g) baby spinach

Meyer lemon slices for garnish

To make the relish, scoop out about half of the pulp from each lemon piece and discard. Coarsely chop the pieces, then put them in a food processor or blender with the shallot and parsley. Pulse several times until minced but not puréed. Transfer to a bowl and stir in the sugar, coriander seeds, and vinegar. Season with salt and pepper, using ½ teaspoon of each. Set aside. (The relish can be made up to 2 days ahead and stored, covered, in the refrigerator; bring to room temperature before serving.)

To make the vinaigrette, in a small nonreactive saucepan, combine the lemon juice, lime juice, and shallot and let stand for 10 minutes. Place the pan over medium-high heat, bring to a simmer, and cook until the mixture is reduced to about ¾ cup (6 fl oz/180 ml), 3–4 minutes. Remove from the heat. Add the oil and whisk until blended. Season to taste with salt and pepper and set aside.

Rinse and dry the scallops. In a frying pan large enough to hold all of the scallops in a single layer without crowding, warm the oil over medium-high heat. When the oil is hot, add the scallops and sear, turning once, until golden, about 30 seconds on each side. Add the wine, stock, vinegar, salt, and pepper. Reduce the heat to low and turn the scallops in the sauce until just opaque throughout, about 45 seconds. Remove from the heat and set aside.

Place the spinach in a bowl, drizzle with the vinaigrette, and toss to coat. Divide the spinach among 8 salad plates and top each with 2 scallops. Alternatively, use 16 scallop shells, placing a few spinach leaves and 1 scallop in each shell and arranging the shells on a large platter or tray. Add a dollop of the Meyer lemon relish to each plate or shell, drizzle the scallops with any remaining pan juices, and garnish with lemon slices. Serve at once.

Pickled ginger imparts a crisp zing to this light and refreshing appetizer. Here, the cucumber slice is a base for the crab topping, but you can also put the cucumber on a cracker or baguette slice and then top with the crab.

Cucumbers with Pickled Ginger and Crab

serves 10–12

6 cucumbers

2 ½ tablespoons mayonnaise

2 teaspoons extra-virgin olive oil

1 ½ teaspoons fresh lemon juice

2 teaspoons minced shallot

1 teaspoon Thai chile paste

1 teaspoon minced fresh chives

¼ teaspoon salt

1 ½ cups (9 oz/280 g) fresh-cooked lump crabmeat, picked over for cartilage and shell fragments, chilled

1 cup (8 oz/250 g) drained sliced pickled ginger

Small fresh flat-leaf (Italian) parsley sprigs for garnish (optional)

serving tip

Thread a bamboo skewer or cocktail pick through the cucumber and crabmeat to make an easy-to-handle party appetizer.

Carefully cut the cucumbers into thin slices ¼ inch (6 mm) thick. You should have about 48 slices.

In a bowl, combine the mayonnaise, olive oil, lemon juice, shallot, chile paste, chives, and salt and mix well. Add the crabmeat and turn gently with a fork to mix well, being careful not to break up the crabmeat too much. Put a generous teaspoonful of the crab mixture on each cucumber round, top with a little of the pickled ginger, and garnish with a parsley sprig, if desired.

Arrange on a platter, cover, and refrigerate for at least 1 hour and up to 2 hours before serving.

The smoky taste of salmon paired with the sea-brine character of caviar makes a delicious combination. True caviar, such as beluga or osetra, is very expensive. But other, less costly fish roe, such as salmon or whitefish, can be used here.

Smoked Salmon Canapés with Caviar

serves 6–8

1 lb (500 g) smoked salmon

2 cups (16 oz/500 g) crème fraîche

½ cup (4 fl oz/125 ml) Sauvignon Blanc, Verdicchio, or other dry white wine

2 tablespoons cider vinegar

2 tablespoons minced shallots

1 tablespoon Dijon mustard

½ teaspoon salt

½ teaspoon freshly ground white pepper

2 tablespoons fresh lemon juice

½ cup (¾ oz/20 g) minced fresh chives

Toasted thin baguette slices or crackers for serving

2 oz (60 g) caviar of choice

Separate the salmon into chunks and set aside.

In a saucepan over medium-high heat, combine the crème fraîche, wine, vinegar, shallots, mustard, salt, and pepper and stir to mix. Bring to a simmer and cook, stirring, until the mixture is reduced by half, 6–7 minutes. Add the salmon, reduce the heat to low, and cook until the fish easily flakes with a fork, about 5 minutes longer. Add the lemon juice and remove from the heat.

Using 2 forks, pull the fish into fine bits, then stir to mix until a thick paste forms. Stir in the chives. Pack snugly into a shallow ramekin, cover, and refrigerate until firm, at least 6 hours and up to 24 hours.

To assemble, spoon a tablespoon of the chilled spread on a baguette slice and top with ¼ teaspoon of caviar. Serve at once.

These layered crostini are perfect for a special occasion. All of the components, including the beef, can be prepared the day before. Then the day of the party, the crostini can be assembled up to 1 hour in advance.

Beef Crostini with Horseradish and Watercress

serves 15–20

2 large baguettes, cut on the diagonal into slices ¼ inch (6 mm) thick

4 tablespoons (2 fl oz/60 ml) extra-virgin olive oil

2–2 ½-lb (1–1.25-kg) piece beef tenderloin, trimmed of fat and sinew

1 ½ teaspoons sea salt

1 tablespoon freshly ground pepper

1 cup (8 oz/250 g) prepared horseradish

2 tablespoons heavy (double) cream

2 bunches watercress, separated into leaves and small sprigs

preparation tip

Half-and-half (half cream) or low-fat plain yogurt can be substituted for the heavy cream.

Preheat the oven to 350°F (180°C).

Arrange the baguette slices in a single layer on 1 or 2 baking sheets and brush with 2 tablespoons of the olive oil. Place in the oven and toast until lightly golden, about 15 minutes. Turn over and toast until the second sides are dry, 7–10 minutes longer. Remove and let cool. (The toasts can be made up to 24 hours ahead. Store at room temperature in an airtight container.)

Raise the oven temperature to 450°F (230°C). Place a rack in a shallow roasting pan just large enough to accommodate the beef tenderloin. Rub the beef all over with the remaining 2 tablespoons olive oil, the salt, and the pepper and place on the rack.

Roast until an instant-read thermometer inserted into the thickest part of the tenderloin registers 115°–120°F (46°–49°C) for rare, about 20 minutes; 125°–130°F (52°–54°C) for medium-rare, about 25 minutes; or 135°–140°F (57°–60°C) for medium, about 30 minutes. Transfer to a cutting board and tent with aluminum foil. Let rest for about 15 minutes. Carve against the grain into paper-thin slices. (The beef can be roasted up to 24 hours ahead. Wrap the tenderloin tightly and refrigerate. Carve the beef cold and then let it come to room temperature before serving.)

In a small bowl, combine the horseradish and cream and mix well.

To assemble, lay a slice or two of beef on a toasted baguette slice. Add a dollop of the horseradish cream and a few leaves or a small sprig of watercress. Arrange on a platter, garnish with more watercress sprigs, and serve.

This elegant appetizer, with its minty tapenade, is a reminder of how well lamb and mint go together. The tapenade can be made up to 2 days in advance and refrigerated, and then brought to room temperature before serving.

Grilled Lamb Chops with Olive-Mint Tapenade

serves 8

OLIVE-MINT TAPENADE

½ lb (250 g) not-too-salty, brine-cured green olives, drained and pitted

½ cup (½ oz/15 g) fresh mint leaves

¼ cup (1 ½ oz/45 g) whole blanched almonds

2 teaspoons capers

2 anchovy fillets

1 teaspoon minced fresh thyme

½ teaspoon fresh lemon juice

1–2 tablespoons extra-virgin olive oil

16 lamb rib chops, about 3 lb (1.5 kg) total weight

1 ½ tablespoons coarse salt

1 tablespoon freshly ground pepper

1 tablespoon chopped fresh thyme

To make the tapenade, in a blender, combine the olives, mint, almonds, capers, anchovies, thyme, and lemon juice and 1 tablespoon of the olive oil and process to a smooth paste. Adjust the consistency with the remaining 1 tablespoon olive oil as needed.

Prepare a fire in a charcoal or gas grill for direct grilling over high heat. Rub the chops all over with the salt, pepper, and thyme.

Place the chops on the grill and cook until seared and golden brown on the first side, about 3 minutes. Turn and grill on the second side, about 3 minutes longer for medium-rare or 4 minutes for medium.

To serve, arrange the chops on a platter and serve hot with the tapenade.

Panini bites are a hearty, kid-friendly appetizer that's easy to vary, depending on the crowd or occasion. Here, Gruyère cheese is used as a common base for three versions. The sandwiches can be assembled up to 6 hours before serving.

Assorted Panini Bites

serves 12–16

8-inch (20-cm) square focaccia, about
1 ½ inches (4 cm) thick

1 ½ tablespoons extra-virgin olive oil

¾ lb (375 g) Gruyère cheese,
thinly sliced

¼ lb (125 g) thinly sliced smoked ham

½ lb (250 g) olive oil–packed roasted red
peppers (capsicums), drained and cut
into strips about 2 inches (5 cm) wide

¼ lb (125 g) thinly sliced roast turkey

2 tablespoons purchased tomato aioli

shopping tip

For added flavor and a touch of
color, use an herbed focaccia,
such as fresh rosemary.

Preheat the oven to 350°F (180°C).

Cut the focaccia crosswise into thirds, then cut each third in half horizontally. You should have 6 pieces each about ½ inches (6 cm) wide, 8 inches (20 cm) long, and ¾ inch (2 cm) thick.

Arrange 3 pieces of the focaccia cut side up on a work surface and drizzle with half of the olive oil. Cover all of the drizzled pieces of focaccia with the cheese slices, dividing them evenly. Cover 1 cheese layer with the ham, another with the red peppers, and the third with the turkey. Drizzle the cut sides of the remaining 3 pieces focaccia with the remaining olive oil, and place 1 on top of the ham and 1 on top of the red peppers, oil side down. Spread the last piece with the aioli and place, aioli side down, on top of the turkey. Using your hands, press down on the tops. Wrap the panini individually in aluminum foil and bake until the cheese melts, about 20 minutes.

Remove from the oven and unwrap. Cut each panino in half lengthwise, and then cut each strip into 8 pieces, each about 1 inch (2.5 cm) square. Arrange on a platter and serve at once.

Tender filet mignon bites glazed with a balsamic reduction and served warm make a special appetizer. The meat can be cubed and the sauce prepared up to 24 hours ahead. The skewers can be assembled an hour before broiling.

Filet Mignon Skewers with Balsamic Reduction

serves 8

8 wooden bamboo skewers

2 tablespoons unsalted butter, plus ½ teaspoon if reheating

2 tablespoons minced shallots

1 ½ teaspoons sea salt

1 ½ teaspoons freshly ground pepper

1 cup (8 fl oz/250 ml) medium-bodied, fruity red wine such as Pinot Noir

2 tablespoons balsamic vinegar

2 lb (1 kg) filet mignon, trimmed of fat

Fresh rosemary sprigs for garnish (optional)

prep tip

Sturdy rosemary branches, stripped of their leaves except for the tips, make decorative skewers. Select branches that are about 4 inches (10 cm) long.

Soak 8 bamboo skewers in water to cover for at least 30 minutes.

In a small saucepan over medium heat, melt the butter. When it foams, add the shallots and sauté until translucent, about 1 minute. Sprinkle with ½ teaspoon each of the salt and pepper. Raise the heat to high and add the wine. Cook until reduced by half, about 4 minutes. Add the balsamic vinegar and continue cooking until reduced to about a third, about 4 minutes longer. Remove from the heat and set aside. (If making ahead, let the reduction cool, then cover and refrigerate until ready to use. Add the ½ teaspoon butter and reheat gently over medium heat.)

Preheat the broiler (grill). Cut the filet mignon into 1-inch (2.5-cm) cubes. You should have about 24 cubes. Transfer the cubes to a bowl, pour the reduction over them, and turn to coat. Drain the skewers and thread 3 cubes of beef onto each skewer. Arrange the skewers on a broiler pan, spacing them about 1 inch (2.5 cm) apart. Season with the remaining 1 teaspoon each salt and pepper.

Place in the the broiler about 6 inches (15 cm) from the heat source and broil (grill) until just browned, about 3 minutes. Turn and broil until just browned on the second side, about 2 minutes for medium-rare, or 3 minutes for medium. Transfer to a platter, garnish with the rosemary, if desired, and serve hot.

Soups & Salads

Butternut Squash Soup with Ginger Crème Fraîche **120**

White Bean Soup with Rosemary **121**

Ideas for Dressing Up Soup **122**

Homemade Crackers **124**

Rosemary Croutons **125**

Leek Soup with Pancetta and Bread Crumbs **127**

Classic Clam Chowder **128**

Sweet Potato Soup with Cheddar and Caviar Croutons **129**

Mixed Greens and Fennel with Ricotta Salata **130**

133 Radicchio Salad with Pears, Walnuts, and Goat Cheese

134 Citrus Salad with Mint and Marcona Almonds

134 Watercress Salad with Apple, Celery, and Blue Cheese

135 Spinach Salad with Orange and Roasted Beets

137 Butter Lettuce Salad with Avocado and Shrimp

138 Smoked Trout and Chicory Salad

139 Wild Rice Salad

140 Israeli Couscous with Squash, Feta, and Almonds

Butternut Squash Soup with Ginger Crème Fraîche

serves 8

2 butternut, acorn, or delicata squashes, 5–6 lb (2.5–3 kg) total weight

6 tablespoons (3 oz/90 g) unsalted butter

1 tablespoon plus 2 ½ teaspoons coarse salt

¾ teaspoon freshly ground black pepper

1 head garlic, cloves separated

4 *each* fresh thyme and rosemary sprigs

1 cup (8 oz/250g) crème fraîche

1 tablespoon peeled and grated fresh ginger

⅛ teaspoon sugar

Pinch of salt

1 cup (5 oz/155 g) chopped shallots

4 cups (32 fl oz/1 l) chicken stock

¾ cup (6 fl oz/180 ml) dry white wine

1 cup (8 fl oz/250 ml) heavy (double) cream

1 teaspoon freshly grated nutmeg

⅛ teaspoon cayenne pepper

Rosemary Croutons (page 125), optional

Photo on page 122

Preheat the oven to 375°F (190°C). Cut each squash in half lengthwise and scoop out the seeds with a spoon. Melt 2 tablespoons of the butter, and brush on the cut surfaces. Sprinkle the cut surfaces with ½ teaspoon each of the salt and black pepper. Stuff the cavities with the unpeeled garlic cloves and 1 sprig each of the thyme and rosemary, then carefully turn the squash halves cut side down on a rimmed baking sheet. Bake until very tender when pierced with a knife, 45–50 minutes. Set aside to cool.

While the squashes are cooking, make the ginger crème fraîche. In a small bowl, stir together the crème fraîche, ginger, sugar, and salt until well blended. Cover and refrigerate until needed.

When the squash halves are cool enough to handle, remove the garlic and herbs and discard the herbs but set the garlic aside. Scoop the flesh out into a bowl. Squeeze the roasted garlic from its skin into the same bowl. In a large pot over medium-high heat, melt the remaining 4 tablespoons (2 oz/60 g) butter. Add the shallots and cook, stirring often, until softened, 3–4 minutes. Add the squash and garlic to the pot and, using the back of a spoon, mash all the ingredients together. Stir in the chicken stock and wine and bring to a simmer. Stir in the cream and remove from the heat.

Using an immersion blender, purée the soup in the pot. Alternatively, purée in batches in a blender or food processor and return the soup to the pot. Add the nutmeg, the cayenne, and the remaining 1 tablespoon plus 2 teaspoons salt and ¼ teaspoon black pepper. Reheat gently to serving temperature if needed. Taste and adjust the seasoning.

To serve, ladle the soup into warmed bowls, add a dollop of ginger crème fraîche, and float a few croutons on top, if desired. Serve hot.

White Bean Soup with Rosemary

serves 10–12

8 qt (8 l) water

2 lb (1 kg) dried cannellini, white kidney, flageolet, or white lima beans

4 fresh rosemary sprigs, plus 1 tablespoon minced leaves and extra sprigs for garnish

1 tablespoon plus 1 teaspoon sea salt

3 tablespoons extra-virgin olive oil

1 ½ small yellow onions, minced

3 ½ qt (3.5 l) chicken stock

1 teaspoon freshly ground pepper

2 bay leaves

prep tip

You can make the soup up to 1 day in advance, cover, and refrigerate. You will need to add an extra 1 cup (8 fl oz/250 ml) stock when reheating. For a heartier soup, add sliced cooked Italian sausages when you stir in the beans. For an alternative garnish, top with grated Parmesan cheese or thinly slivered fried vegetables (page 122).

Photo on page 123

In a large pot, combine the water, the beans, the 4 rosemary sprigs, and the 1 tablespoon salt and bring to a boil over medium-high heat. Reduce the heat to low, cover partially, and simmer until the beans are tender to the bite, 2–2 ½ hours. Using a slotted spoon, transfer the beans to a bowl and set aside, reserving the cooking liquid in the pot. You should have about 8 cups (64 fl oz/2 l) liquid remaining. Add more water or return the bean broth to a gentle boil and cook until reduced as needed for 8 cups.

In another pot over medium heat, warm the olive oil. When the oil is hot, add the onions and sauté until translucent, 3–4 minutes. Add the chicken stock, the reserved cooking liquid, the pepper, the 1 teaspoon salt, the bay leaves, and the minced rosemary. Raise the heat to high and bring to a boil. Reduce the heat to low and simmer, uncovered, until the flavors are well blended, about 30 minutes.

Discard the bay leaves, stir in the beans, and cook for 5 minutes longer. Taste and adjust the seasoning. Ladle the soup into warmed bowls and garnish with the rosemary sprigs. Serve hot.

Ideas for Dressing Up Soup

drizzle of crème fraîche

A zigzag of herb-flecked crème fraîche and
a pair of long-stemmed chive buds make an
elegant topping for a puréed soup. Or, use a
dollop of yogurt, sour cream, goat cheese, or
flavored whipped cream with green garlic, a
sprig of rosemary, or a spray of sage leaves.

caviar and croutons

Croutons add crunch, flavor, and eye appeal
to soups. Combine them with a spoonful
of crème fraîche, a dollop of caviar, and a
sprinkle of fresh herbs. For a variation, try
salmon roe and fresh dill.

fried vegetables and herbs

A handful of root vegetables, thinly sliced
and fried, is a colorful topping for soup. Use
any baby vegetable, such as beets, fennel,
artichokes, carrot, parsnip, or celery root
(celeriac). Trim and peel as needed, then
thinly slice with a paring knife or mandoline.
In a small frying pan over medium heat,
warm canola oil to a depth of ½ inch (12 mm)
just until it smokes. Fry the vegetables in
small batches until golden. Drain on paper
towels until cool and crisp, then season with
salt. Place a handful of vegetables on each
serving, and sprinkle with fresh herbs.

Homemade crackers add a special touch and salty crunch to any soup but are particularly delicious with chowder. You can make the crackers up to 2 days ahead and store them at room temperature in an airtight container.

Homemade Crackers

makes 60–70 crackers

1 package (2 ½ teaspoons)
active dry yeast

¼ cup (2 fl oz/60 ml) warm water
(105°–115°F/40°–46°C)

¾ cup (6 fl oz/180 ml) whole milk

2 tablespoons unsalted butter,
at room temperature

1 tablespoon sugar

1 teaspoon kosher salt

1 large egg

1 ½ tablespoons fennel seeds

3 ½–4 cups (17 ½–20 oz/545–625 g)
all-purpose (plain) flour

Coarse sea salt for sprinkling

In a large bowl, dissolve the yeast in the warm water and let stand until foamy, about 5 minutes. In a medium saucepan over medium heat, heat the milk until small bubbles appear around the edges of the pan. Remove from the heat and stir in the butter, sugar, and salt.

Let the milk mixture cool to lukewarm. Using a whisk, beat in the egg and fennel seeds until blended. Add to the yeast mixture. Add 2 cups (10 oz/315 g) of the flour and beat with a wooden spoon until smooth, about 3 minutes. Add 1 ½ cups (7 ½ oz/230 g) of the flour and beat until the dough is moderately soft, 2–3 minutes longer. If the dough seems too soft, add more flour.

Turn the dough out onto a lightly floured work surface and knead until smooth and elastic, 5–6 minutes. Shape into a ball, place in a lightly buttered bowl, and then turn the ball to coat. Cover the bowl with a damp kitchen towel and let the dough rise in a warm place until doubled in bulk, about 1 hour.

Punch down the dough, re-cover, and let rest for 10 minutes. Meanwhile, preheat the oven to 450°F (230°C). Sprinkle a rimmed baking sheet with flour.

Divide the dough into balls about the size of large olives. On a lightly floured work surface, roll out each ball into a paper-thin round 2 inches (5 cm) in diameter and place on the prepared pan. Sprinkle each round with coarse salt, and then prick the crackers with fork tines to prevent puffing.

Place the sheet in the oven and bake for 5 minutes. Turn over the crackers and continue baking until lightly browned on both sides, about 5 minutes longer. Puncture any air bubbles with fork tines and let cool on the pan. Repeat with the remaining dough balls.

These flavorful croutons are quick to make and a perfect accompaniment for vegetable soups and for salads. You can substitute almost any fresh herb, such as thyme, tarragon, or oregano for the rosemary.

Rosemary Croutons

makes about 60 croutons

10 slices coarse country bread, ½ inch (12 mm) thick

4 tablespoons (2 oz/60 g) unsalted butter, melted

2 fresh rosemary sprigs

½ teaspoon coarse salt

¼ teaspoon freshly ground pepper

prep tip

The croutons can be made up to 2 days in advance and stored in an airtight container at room temperature.

Preheat the oven to 350°F (180°C).

Cut the bread slices into ½-inch (12-mm) cubes and place in a large bowl. Add the butter, rosemary sprigs, salt, and pepper and stir to coat the bread cubes evenly with the butter. Spread the bread cubes on a rimmed baking sheet.

Bake, stirring once at the midway point, until the cubes are evenly browned and crisp, 15–18 minutes. Remove from the oven, remove and discard the rosemary sprigs, and let the croutons cool before using.

A simple leek soup is dressed up with a topping of crispy pancetta and buttered bread crumbs to make a first course suitable for any holiday meal. It also makes a good lunch or brunch dish, accompanied by a salad.

Leek Soup with Pancetta and Bread Crumbs

serves 8

3 oz (90 g) thinly sliced pancetta, cut into ½-inch (12-mm) pieces

4 tablespoons (2 oz/60 g) unsalted butter

1 cup (2 oz/60 g) fresh bread crumbs

4 leeks, white and tender green parts, finely chopped

2 tablespoons chopped yellow onion

1 rib celery, chopped

1 small potato, peeled and chopped

6 cups (48 fl oz/1.5 l) chicken stock

1 cup (8 fl oz/250 ml) heavy (double) cream

serving tip

For a vegetarian topping, top the soup with buttered bread crumbs and curls of Parmesan cheese.

In a frying pan over medium heat, cook the pancetta, stirring occasionally, until crispy, 4–5 minutes. Transfer to paper towels to drain.

In a saucepan over medium-high heat, melt 2 tablespoons of the butter. When it foams, add the bread crumbs and cook, stirring, until golden brown, about 5 minutes. Transfer to a plate and set aside.

In a large pot, melt the remaining 2 tablespoons butter over medium-high heat. When it foams, add the leeks, onion, celery, and potato and sauté until the leeks and onion are translucent, 3–4 minutes. Add the chicken stock, reduce the heat to low, cover, and simmer until the potato is tender, about 15 minutes. Remove from the heat.

Using an immersion blender, purée the soup in the pot. Alternatively, purée the soup in batches in a blender or food processor. Add the cream, place over medium-high heat, and bring to just under a boil. Let cool, then strain through a fine-mesh sieve lined with cheesecloth (muslin). Transfer the soup to a clean pot and bring to a simmer over low heat. Cook, uncovered, to allow the flavors to blend, about 5 minutes longer.

Ladle into warmed bowls, sprinkle with the pancetta, and garnish with the bread crumbs. Serve hot.

The addition of fennel gives this classic salad of mixed greens a refreshing anise accent, while the simple dressing of olive oil and lemon juice highlights, rather than masks, the individual flavors of all the ingredients.

Mixed Greens and Fennel with Ricotta Salata

serves 8

3 tablespoons extra-virgin olive oil

1 tablespoon fresh lemon juice

½ teaspoon sea salt

½ teaspoon freshly ground pepper

1 head escarole (Batavian endive)

1 head green or red oakleaf lettuce

1 fennel bulb

¼ lb (125 g) *ricotta salata* cheese

shopping tip

You can substitute feta, goat cheese, or pecorino for the *ricotta salata*.

In a large salad bowl, combine the olive oil, lemon juice, salt, and pepper and mix well with a fork or whisk.

Separate the escarole leaves and select the yellow innermost leaves, tearing them into bite-sized pieces; you should have about 3 cups (4 ½ oz/140 g). Separate the oakleaf lettuce leaves, choosing as many of the small leaves as possible to make 3 cups (3 oz/90 g). If you need to use some of the larger leaves, tear them into bite-sized pieces. Reserve the remaining escarole and lettuce leaves for another use.

Cut off the stems and feathery fronds of the fennel bulb and remove any bruised or discolored outer layers. Cut the bulb in half lengthwise and cut out any tough core parts. Using a mandoline or a sharp chef's knife, cut the bulb halves crosswise into slices about ⅛ inch (3 mm) thick. Cut the slices lengthwise into pieces ½ inch (12 mm) wide.

Add the fennel slices, escarole, and lettuce to the salad bowl holding the dressing and toss to coat evenly. Crumble the *ricotta salata* on top and toss again. Serve at once.

Radicchio's brilliant red hues and gentle bitterness are a good foil for sweet pears. Goat cheese and walnuts accompany the radicchio here, but a mild blue cheese paired with almonds or pistachios could be used in their place.

Radicchio Salad with Pears, Walnuts, and Goat Cheese

serves 8

½ cup (2 oz/60 g) walnuts

2 firm but ripe pears

1 tablespoon fresh lemon juice

2 radicchio heads

3 tablespoons extra-virgin olive oil

1 tablespoon plus 2 teaspoons balsamic vinegar

¼ teaspoon salt

6 oz (185 g) soft fresh goat cheese

shopping tip

Look for Treviso, a variety of radicchio with long, narrow leaves and a milder flavor than the more common round Chioggia variety. When buying either type, select good-sized, firm heads with dark leaves and bright white ribs.

Preheat the oven to 350°F (180°C). Place the walnuts in a single layer on a baking sheet and bake, stirring once or twice, until fragrant and lightly toasted, 10–12 minutes. Transfer onto a plate and let cool, then chop coarsely.

Halve and core the pears and then cut lengthwise into thin slices. Drizzle with the lemon juice and set aside. Remove and discard any brown or wilted leaves from the radicchio heads, then remove 8 sturdy outer leaves and set aside. Cut the heads in half and cut out and discard the cores. Chop the heads finely.

In a large bowl, combine the olive oil, 1 tablespoon of the vinegar, and the salt and mix well with a fork or whisk. Add the chopped radicchio and toss to coat.

Place a reserved radicchio leaf on each salad plate. Spoon the dressed and chopped radicchio onto the leaves, dividing it evenly and partially filling each leaf. Arrange pear slices on the radicchio. Crumble the goat cheese on top and sprinkle with the walnuts. Drizzle each salad plate evenly with the 2 teaspoons balsamic vinegar and serve at once.

Citrus Salad with Mint and Marcona Almonds

serves 8

1 tablespoon honey

1 tablespoon fresh orange juice

½ teaspoon fresh lemon juice

2 tablespoons minced fresh mint,
plus leaves for garnish

3 grapefruits

3 navel oranges

12 kumquats

8 butter (Boston) lettuce leaves

¼ cup (1 ½ oz/45 g) Marcona almonds

In a large bowl, combine the honey, orange juice, lemon juice, and minced mint and mix well with a fork or whisk.

Working with 1 grapefruit at a time, cut a slice from the top and bottom to reveal the flesh. Stand the grapefruit upright and slice downward to remove the peel and white pith. Holding the grapefruit in one hand, cut along either side of each segment to release it from the membrane, letting the segments drop into a bowl. Remove any seeds, cut the segments in half, and add to the honey mixture along with any juices. Repeat the process with the oranges. Cut the kumquats in half lengthwise, remove the seeds, and also add to the bowl. Gently turn the fruit to coat with the dressing.

Place a lettuce leaf on each salad plate and divide the fruit among them. Sprinkle with the almonds, garnish with the mint leaves, and serve.

Watercress Salad with Apple, Celery, and Blue Cheese

serves 8

¼ cup *each* (2 fl oz/60 ml) mayonnaise
and nonfat plain yogurt

1 tablespoon cider vinegar

1 tablespoon whole milk

¼ lb (125 g) Maytag or other mild blue
cheese, crumbled

3 mild, sweet red apples such as Gala

2 cups (2 oz/60 g) watercress
leaves, plus sprigs for garnish

4 ribs celery, chopped

In a bowl, combine the mayonnaise, yogurt, vinegar, and milk and mix well with a fork. Add one-fourth of the cheese and, using the fork, mash it into the mayonnaise mixture to make a dressing.

Halve, core, and cube the apples. In a large bowl, combine the apples, watercress leaves, and celery and toss to mix. Spoon the dressing over the apple mixture and toss gently to coat. Divide the salad among individual plates and garnish with the watercress sprigs and the remaining cheese.

Plump, sweet navel oranges turn up frequently in winter salads—and not just in fruit salads. They add appealing color and tang to this mix of beets and spinach, a good prelude to a main course of pork chops or duck.

Spinach Salad with Orange and Roasted Beets

serves 6

4 small beets, about ½ lb (250 g) total weight

2 large navel oranges

6 cups (6 oz/185 g) baby spinach

DRESSING

3 tablespoons extra-virgin olive oil

1 tablespoon fresh lemon juice, plus more to taste

1 shallot, minced

Salt and freshly ground pepper

shopping tip

Red-fleshed blood oranges, delicious during winter, can be used in place of the navel oranges.

Photo on page 59

Preheat the oven to 375°F (190°C). Remove the beet greens from the beets, leaving 1 inch (2.5 cm) of stem intact (reserve the greens for another use). Place the beets in a baking dish and add water to a depth of ¼ inch (6 mm). Cover and bake until tender when pierced with a knife, 45–60 minutes.

Working with 1 orange at a time, cut a slice from the top and bottom to reveal the flesh. Stand the orange upright and thickly slice downward to remove the peel and white pith. Holding the orange in one hand, cut along either side of each segment to release it from the membrane, letting the segments drop into a bowl. Repeat with the remaining orange. Put the spinach in a large bowl.

To make the dressing, in a small bowl, whisk together the olive oil, 1 tablespoon lemon juice, and shallot. Season to taste with salt and pepper. Let stand for about 30 minutes to allow the flavor of the shallot to mellow.

When the beets are done, remove from the oven and let stand until cool enough to handle. Peel and cut into wedges about the size of the orange sections. Put the beet wedges in a bowl and toss with just enough of the dressing to coat them lightly.

Using a slotted spoon, transfer the orange sections to the bowl holding the spinach. (Reserve any collected juice for another use.) Add the remaining dressing and toss to coat. Taste and adjust the seasoning with salt, pepper, and lemon juice.

Divide the spinach and oranges among individual plates. Arrange the beets on top, dividing them evenly. Serve at once.

Tangerine vinaigrette, made with dual flavors of fresh juice and infused oil, adds a sweet, almost tropical accent to this simple, colorful salad. The flavored olive oil is available in gourmet markets.

Butter Lettuce Salad with Avocado and Shrimp

serves 8

1 tablespoon black peppercorns

1 tablespoon coriander seeds

1 ½ teaspoons sea salt

1 ½ lb (750 g) medium shrimp (prawns), peeled and deveined with tail segments intact

2 heads butter (Boston) lettuce

2 avocados, halved, pitted, peeled, and diced

¼ cup (2 fl oz/60 ml) tangerine-infused olive oil

1 tablespoon fresh tangerine juice

1 tablespoon sherry vinegar

¼ teaspoon freshly ground white pepper

shopping tip

To save time, purchase ready-cooked shrimp; rinse, drain, and pat dry before adding them to the salad.

Fill a large saucepan three-fourths full of water; add the peppercorns, the coriander seeds, and 1 teaspoon of the salt; and bring to almost a simmer over medium-high heat. Reduce the heat to low and carefully add the shrimp. Cook until just opaque throughout, 45–60 seconds. Drain in a colander, rinse with cold water, and set aside.

Separate the lettuce leaves, tearing large leaves in halves or quarters and leaving small leaves whole. Divide the lettuce among salad plates. Top with the avocados and shrimp, dividing them evenly.

In a small bowl, combine the olive oil, tangerine juice, vinegar, the remaining ½ teaspoon salt, and the white pepper and mix well with a fork or whisk. Pour an equal amount of the vinaigrette over each salad and serve at once.

Smoked trout, readily available in most supermarkets, needs only a little endive and a light dressing to bring out its subtle flavor. Serve this salad as a starter, or pair with fresh bread and a chocolate dessert for a light meal.

Smoked Trout and Chicory Salad

serves 8

3 tablespoons extra-virgin olive oil

1 tablespoon Champagne vinegar

2 teaspoons grated lemon zest

½ teaspoon sea salt

½ teaspoon freshly ground pepper

2 heads chicory (curly endive)

1 cup (1 oz/30 g) fresh flat-leaf
(Italian) parsley leaves

1 lb (500 g) smoked trout fillet

8 lemon slices for garnish

shopping tip

For a crunchier salad, substitute 6 heads Belgian endive (chicory/witloof), torn into bite-sized pieces, for the chicory. Cut ½ inch (12 mm) off the stem end and separate the leaves.

In a large bowl, combine the olive oil, vinegar, lemon zest, salt, and pepper and mix well with a fork or whisk.

Separate the chicory leaves and select the yellow and pale green inner leaves. Tear the leaves into bite-sized pieces. Put the chicory and the parsley leaves in the bowl with the vinaigrette and toss to coat.

Using two forks, tear the trout into bite-sized pieces and add to the bowl. Toss gently once or twice to mix.

To serve, mound the salad onto chilled salad plates. Garnish each salad with a lemon slice and serve at once.

Cooking the mushrooms separately and then folding them into the rice lets them contribute their own distinctive aroma to the dish. You can use shiitakes or chanterelles instead of button mushrooms, or a mixture.

Wild Rice Salad

serves 10–12

6 celery ribs

3 tablespoons extra-virgin olive oil

½ cup (2 ½ oz/75 g) finely chopped yellow onion

2 cups (12 oz/375 g) wild rice

1 tablespoon minced fresh flat-leaf (Italian) parsley

1 teaspoon minced fresh sage

1 teaspoon salt

¾ teaspoon freshly ground pepper

6 cups (48 fl oz/1.5 l) chicken stock

1 tablespoon unsalted butter

½ lb (250 g) button mushrooms, brushed clean and sliced

Trim the celery ribs and cut each rib crosswise into 2-inch (5-cm) lengths. Then cut the pieces lengthwise on a slight angle to make long slivers about ¼ inch (6 mm) wide. Set aside.

In a large saucepan over medium heat, warm the olive oil. When the oil is hot, add the onion and celery and sauté until soft, 7–8 minutes. Add the wild rice, parsley, sage, ¾ teaspoon of the salt, and ½ teaspoon of the pepper and stir until the rice glistens, 1–2 minutes. Pour in the chicken stock, raise the heat to high, and bring to a boil. Reduce the heat to medium-low, cover, and cook until the wild rice is tender, about 50 minutes.

About 5 minutes before the rice is ready, cook the mushrooms. In a frying pan over medium-high heat, melt the butter. When it foams, add the mushrooms and sauté until lightly golden, about 5 minutes. Season with the remaining ¼ teaspoon each salt and pepper.

When the rice is done, drain off any excess liquid and stir in the hot mushrooms. Transfer to a warmed bowl and serve hot.

Israeli couscous is larger and more substantial than the familiar North African variety and makes an excellent base for an unusual pasta salad with a bounty of flavorful ingredients. Serve this as a first course, or part of a holiday buffet.

Israeli Couscous with Squash, Feta, and Almonds

serves 8

¾ cup (3 ½ oz/90 g) almonds

1 tablespoon chopped fresh sage

2 teaspoons salt

1 teaspoon ground cinnamon

1 teaspoon chili powder

1 teaspoon freshly ground pepper

2 acorn squashes, about 2 ½ lb
(1.25 kg) total weight

1 tablespoon extra-virgin olive oil,
plus extra for drizzling

2 cups (12 oz/375 g) Israeli couscous

6 oz (185 g) feta cheese, crumbled

¼ cup (¼ oz/7 g) minced fresh mint,
plus sprigs for garnish

Preheat the oven to 350°F (180°C). Place the almonds in a single layer on a baking sheet and bake, stirring once or twice, until fragrant and lightly toasted, 10–12 minutes. Transfer to a plate and let cool. Leave the oven on.

In a small bowl, combine the sage, 1 teaspoon of the salt, the cinnamon, the chili powder, and the pepper and mix well.

Peel the squashes. Cut each squash crosswise into rings about 1 inch (2.5 cm) thick and discard the seeds. Rub the cut sides with the 1 tablespoon olive oil. Arrange the rings on a baking sheet and rub both sides with the sage mixture. Roast until lightly browned and easily pierced with a knife, about 1 hour. Cut each ring into 4 sections.

Rinse the couscous in cold water and let drain in a colander for about 10 minutes. Fill a saucepan half full with water and bring to a boil. Add the couscous and cook until tender, about 20 minutes. Drain in the colander.

Transfer the couscous to a warmed platter. Drizzle with a little olive oil and gently fluff, separating the grains with your fingertips. Season with the remaining 1 teaspoon salt, then taste and adjust the seasoning.

To serve, sprinkle the couscous with the feta cheese, almonds, and minced mint. Turn gently to distribute the ingredients, and then fold in the squash. Garnish with the mint sprigs and serve warm or at room temperature.

Mains

Risotto with Porcini Mushrooms **144**

Crab Soufflé **145**

Fresh Cracked Crab with Chile Dipping Sauce **147**

True Cod Fillets with Shallot and Meyer Lemon Sauce **148**

Smoked Salmon Fillet with Toppings **151**

Preparing the Turkey **153**

Ideas for Garnishing the Turkey **155**

Tarragon-Stuffed Chicken with Pan Gravy **156**

Turkey Breast with Bacon, Oregano, and Peppers **157**

Roast Turkey Seasoned with Sage **158**

160 Mushroom Stuffing with Herbs and Cranberries

161 Cider-Shallot Pan Gravy

162 Grilled Turkey with Maple Glaze

163 Sausage, Apple, and Thyme Stuffing

165 Rack of Lamb with Garlic and Herbs

166 Baked Ham with Spiced Cider Glaze

168 Roast Pork Loin with Salt-and-Fennel Rub

169 Filet Mignon with Red Currant and Wine Sauce

171 Rosemary Rib Roast with Yorkshire Pudding

Carnaroli rice, a short-grain variety grown in Italy, has the perfect texture for this dish, although Italian Arborio rice is an excellent second choice. Risotto is traditionally made with broth, but this recipe is so rich that water can be used.

Risotto with Porcini Mushrooms

serves 4

²/₃ cup (²/₃ oz/20 g) dried porcini mushrooms (ceps)

1 ½ cups (12 fl oz/375 g) lukewarm water

4 cups (32 fl oz/1 l) chicken stock

2 tablespoons olive oil

2 tablespoons finely chopped shallots

1 ½ cups (10 ½ oz/330 g) Carnaroli or Arborio rice

½ cup (4 fl oz/125 ml) dry white wine such as Pinot Grigio

¼ cup (1 oz/30 g) grated Parmesan cheese, preferably Parmigiano-Reggiano

Kosher salt and freshly ground pepper

serving tip

This risotto also makes a good first course served in smaller portions for up to six people.

Place the mushrooms in a bowl with the water and let soak until soft, 20–30 minutes. Lift out the mushrooms, reserving the soaking liquid. Squeeze the mushrooms dry and chop them. Strain the soaking liquid through a fine-mesh sieve lined with cheesecloth (muslin). Reserve ½ cup (4 fl oz/125 ml) for the risotto. Save the remaining liquid for another use.

In a saucepan over medium heat, warm the chicken stock until bubbles appear around the edges of the pan. Adjust the heat to maintain a gentle simmer.

In a deep, heavy saucepan over medium-high heat, warm 1 tablespoon of the olive oil. Add the shallots and sauté until translucent, about 2 minutes. Add the remaining olive oil and stir in the rice. Reduce the heat to medium and cook, stirring, until the rice is coated with the oil and the grains turn translucent at the edges, about 1 minute. Pour in the wine and stir for 2–3 minutes.

Add ½ cup (4 fl oz/125 ml) of the hot stock and cook, stirring occasionally, until most of the liquid has been absorbed and the rice is just moist, about 3 minutes. Continue adding stock, ½ cup at a time, waiting until the rice is just moist before adding more. After 2 cups (16 fl oz/500 ml) stock have been used, add the ½ cup mushroom soaking liquid and the chopped mushrooms. When the liquid is almost fully absorbed, resume adding the stock.

The risotto is ready when it is creamy and slightly soupy, about 35 minutes after the first addition of stock. Remove from the heat.

Stir in the cheese and season to taste with salt and pepper. Divide evenly among warmed shallow bowls or plates and serve at once.

This dish has a sophisticated flavor and appearance both impressive and appealing. To showcase the crab, keep the rest of the meal simple, preceding the soufflé with a salad and finishing with a chocolate dessert.

Crab Soufflé

serves 4

4 tablespoons (2 oz/60 g) unsalted butter

1 tablespoon grated Parmesan cheese

4 large eggs, separated, plus 2 large egg whites

2 tablespoons minced shallots

¼ cup (1 ½ oz/45 g) all-purpose (plain) flour

1 teaspoon salt

¼ teaspoon freshly ground black pepper

⅛ teaspoon cayenne pepper

1 cup (8 fl oz/250 ml) whole milk

1 cup (6 oz/185 g) fresh-cooked lump crabmeat, picked over for cartilage and shell fragments, coarsely torn or chopped

Preheat the oven to 375°F (190°C).

Use ½ tablespoon of the butter to grease a 1-qt (1-l) soufflé dish. Sprinkle the bottom with the cheese, then turn the dish on its side and tap and turn it to coat the sides with the cheese.

In a bowl, using an electric mixer, beat the 6 egg whites until stiff peaks form, about 4 minutes. In another bowl, using the electric mixer, beat the 4 egg yolks until creamy, about 2 minutes. Set the whites and yolks aside separately.

In a saucepan over medium-high heat, melt the remaining 3 ½ tablespoons butter. When it foams, add the shallots and sauté until translucent, about 1 minute. Remove from the heat and whisk in the flour, salt, black pepper, and cayenne. Return to the heat and slowly add the milk, whisking constantly. Cook, stirring often, until smooth and thickened, about 5 minutes. Remove from the heat and let cool for 2–3 minutes.

Whisk the egg yolks into the white sauce until well blended. Stir in the crab.

Stir 3 tablespoons of the egg whites into the crab mixture to lighten it. Using a spatula, gently fold in the remaining egg whites just until combined. Spoon the mixture gently into the prepared dish. Bake until the top has puffed and is golden brown, about 40 minutes.

Serve at once, scooping the soufflé directly from its baking dish.

Cracking crab around a dinner table makes for a festive meal. Be sure to supply crab-cracking tools and bowls for the spent shells. Make plenty of the sauce, too. Adults and children alike will appreciate its spicy taste.

Fresh Cracked Crab with Chile Dipping Sauce

serves 8

4–6 cooked Dungeness crabs

CHILE DIPPING SAUCE

4 cups (32 fl oz/1 l) mayonnaise

½ cup (4 oz/125 g) Thai chile paste

3 tablespoons minced shallots

2 sweet pickles, minced

3 tablespoons sweet pickle juice

2 teaspoons cayenne pepper

2 teaspoons Worcestershire sauce

½–1 teaspoon salt

½–1 cup (4–8 fl oz/125–250 ml) half-and-half (half cream) or whole milk

Lemon wedges for garnish

serving tip

Put out small damp towels and lemon slices for guests to clean their hands after eating the crab.

Working with 1 crab at a time, break the claws and legs off and crack each segment. Put the body on its back and push down on each side to break it out of the shell. Remove the gills and viscera and rinse the body well. Break the body in half down its centerline. Cover and refrigerate the crab until ready to serve. Alternatively, many markets will crack and clean the crab for you.

To make the dipping sauce, in a large bowl, combine the mayonnaise, chile paste, shallots, pickles, pickle juice, and cayenne. Add the Worcestershire sauce, ½ teaspoon salt, and ½ cup half-and-half. Taste and add more salt if needed. If the sauce is too stiff, thin with a little more of the half-and-half. Transfer to 1 or 2 small serving bowls.

Arrange the crab on 1 or 2 platters and tuck the lemon wedges around the edge. Serve the bowl(s) on the platter(s) or alongside.

True cod is one of only a few existing bona fide species of cod, unlike many other fish that go by the name, such as rock cod and lingcod. Also called Pacific cod and gray cod, it is a lean, firm, mild-flavored white fish.

True Cod Fillets with Shallot and Meyer Lemon Sauce

serves 8

2 teaspoons sea salt

8 skinless true cod fillets, each about 6 oz (185 g) and ½ inch (12 mm) thick

2 teaspoons freshly ground white pepper

½ cup (4 fl oz/125 ml) dry white wine such as Sauvignon Blanc

6 tablespoons (3 oz/90 g) unsalted butter, cut into 1-tablespoon pieces

2 tablespoons minced shallots

1 tablespoon grated Meyer lemon zest

2 tablespoons fresh Meyer lemon juice

2 tablespoons heavy (double) cream

prep tip

You can flavor the sauce with other citrus, such as orange, tangerine, or lime, in place of the Meyer lemon.

Place a large, nonstick frying pan over medium-high heat and sprinkle it with 1 teaspoon of the salt. When the pan is hot, add the cod fillets and sear until opaque and lightly golden on the first side, about 1 minute. Turn and cook on the other side until opaque and lightly golden, about 1 minute longer. Sprinkle with the pepper, pour in the wine, and cover. Reduce the heat to low and cook until the fish is opaque throughout and just flakes with a fork, 1–2 minutes longer. Transfer to a warmed platter and tent with aluminum foil.

In a saucepan over medium-high heat, melt 1 tablespoon of the butter. When it foams, add the shallots and cook until translucent, about 1 minute. Add the lemon zest and juice and the cream and bring to a rolling boil, about 45 seconds. Add the remaining 5 tablespoons (2 ½ oz/75 g) butter and stir until the butter is melted, about 45 seconds longer.

Divide the fillets among warmed plates and drizzle the sauce over or alongside the fish. Serve at once.

Smoking a full side of salmon on a charcoal or gas grill is well worth the effort. You can smoke the fish a day or two in advance, and then cover it well and refrigerate it. Bring the salmon to room temperature before serving.

Smoked Salmon Fillet with Toppings

serves 8–10

1 whole salmon fillet, skin on, about 3 lb (1.5 kg)

1 cup (8 oz/250 g) sea salt

1 cup (7 oz/220 g) firmly packed light brown sugar

1 yellow onion, minced

6 cloves garlic, minced

¼ cup (⅓ oz/10 g) chopped fresh dill

1 tablespoon minced fresh thyme

6 fresh tarragon sprigs, chopped

3 handfuls of wood chips such as apple or mesquite

TOPPINGS

½ cup *each* (4 fl oz/125 ml) mayonnaise and Dijon mustard, mixed with 2 tablespoons prepared horseradish

1 cup (8 oz/250 g) capers

1 cup (6 oz/185 g) minced red onion

Select a roasting pan large enough to hold the fillet and line it with aluminum foil. Place the salmon, skin side down, on the foil. In a bowl, combine the salt, brown sugar, onion, garlic, dill, thyme, and tarragon. Rub the mixture over the surface of the salmon. Cover and refrigerate for 3–4 hours.

Rinse the fish under cold water and pat dry. Place skin side down on a large, clean sheet of foil. Let stand until a sticky coat forms, about 30 minutes.

In a large bowl, soak the wood chips in water to cover for 20 minutes. Prepare a charcoal or gas grill for indirect grilling over medium heat. (For a charcoal grill, pile the coals on either side of the grill grate, leaving the center empty. For a gas grill, turn off half of the burners.)

Drain the wood chips and scatter over the coals. If using a gas grill, put the drained chips in a smoker box, or in a heavy-duty foil packet with a few holes poked in it, and place directly on the lit burner(s). Cover the grill and heat until the chips start to smoke, about 10 minutes.

Place the grill rack 4–6 inches (10–15 cm) from the fire. Trim the edges of the foil, leaving a 1-inch (2.5-cm) overhang on all sides. Place the fish on its foil over the center of the charcoal grill, or over the unlit burner(s) of the gas grill. Re-cover and cook until the salmon is opaque throughout and just flakes with a fork, or until an instant-read thermometer registers 140°F (60°C), 20–25 minutes. Using 2 spatulas, slide the fillet and its foil base onto a warmed platter. Discard the foil.

Serve the salmon on the platter. Accompany with the toppings.

Preparing the Turkey

Turkey is the classic centerpiece of the holiday meal. It can be grilled, roasted, and even deep-fried. Whichever method you choose, the goal is to produce a bird with juicy, tender meat and a crisp, well-browned skin.

thawing

Preferably, buy a fresh turkey. If using a frozen bird, plan on 1 day of thawing in the refrigerator for every 4 to 5 pounds (2 to 2.75 kg). Or, you can thaw the bird in a water bath: Submerge the fully wrapped turkey in cold tap water, and change the water every 30 minutes. Plan on 30 minutes in the water for every pound (500 g) of turkey.

testing for doneness

About 30 minutes before the total roasting time is reached, insert an instant-read thermometer into the thickest part of the thigh away from the bone. The bird is done when the thermometer registers 170°–175°F (77°–80°C). Because the bird's internal temperature will continue to rise outside the oven, remove it from the oven when it is about 5°F (3°C) below the desired temperature.

carving

Set the turkey, breast side up, on the cutting board. Remove the wings by pulling them away from the body to find the shoulder joint and cutting through the joint. Discard each wing tip, and carve each wing at the elbow joint into two pieces. Remove each whole leg with the thigh attached in the same way. Separate each drumstick from the thigh by cutting through the joint. You can serve the drumsticks and thighs whole if the bird is relatively small. If the turkey is large, slice the meat off, cutting parallel to the bone. On each side of the turkey, just above the shoulder and thigh joints, carve a horizontal cut straight through the breast to the bone. Then carve thin slices vertically, cutting straight down to end each slice at the base cut. As you carve the slices, either place them on a platter or serve them directly to the guests.

Ideas for Garnishing the Turkey

pomegranates and figs

For a colorful and rustic presentation, use a mix of fresh or dried fruits. Use a knife to cut a crisscross pattern in the top of 2 or 3 pomegranates, making it just big enough for you to tear each fruit into 2 or 3 sections. The figs can be halved by pulling them apart from the sides. Or use other seasonal fruits, such as persimmons, kumquats, or dates.

olive leaves and blackberries

Olive leaves and berries add a simple elegance to the turkey platter. Use a few small branches of olive leaves and a handful of berries. Other fruits, such as cranberries, dried apricots, or apples, can also be used.

grilled citrus

A mix of citrus, such as lemons, oranges, tangerines, and kumquats, brightens a holiday turkey platter. To grill the citrus, cut the fruits in half and place cut side down on a heated grill until they begin to char. The citrus leaves can also be put on the grill for a minute or two to give them a charred appearance. Also consider grilled apples, pears, or figs.

A big roast turkey is a staple of the holiday table. Here, it is accompanied with a mushroom-rich bread stuffing that includes another seasonal favorite, cranberries, and a simple brandy-scented pan gravy.

Roast Turkey Seasoned with Sage

serves 10–12

1 turkey, 16–18 lb (8–9 kg), neck and giblets removed

Salt and freshly ground pepper

1 yellow onion, cut into 6 wedges, plus 3 large yellow onions, cut into slices ½ inch (12 mm) thick

8–10 fresh sage leaves

2 tablespoons unsalted butter, at room temperature

Mushroom Stuffing with Herbs and Cranberries (page 160)

Cider-Shallot Pan Gravy (page 161)

Remove the turkey from the refrigerator about 1 hour before roasting. Position a rack in the lower third of the oven and preheat the oven to 325°F (165°C). Remove and discard any pockets of fat from the cavity.

Season the cavity with salt and pepper, and add the onion wedges and sage. Tie the legs together with kitchen string, if desired. Tuck the wing tips under the back and tie a length of string around the breast to hold the wings close to the body. Rub the butter over the turkey breast. Select a roasting pan just large enough to hold the turkey. Place the sliced onions in the middle to form a natural roasting rack, and put the turkey, breast side up, on top.

Roast the turkey until an instant-read thermometer inserted into the thickest part of a thigh away from the bone registers 170°–175°F (77°–80° C), 3 ½–4 hours.

When the turkey is done, transfer it to a platter or carving board, remove the strings, and loosely tent with aluminum foil. Let rest for 15–20 minutes. If desired, spoon the fat off the pan drippings and reserve the pan juices for making the gravy.

Discard the contents of the turkey cavity and carve the turkey (page 152). Serve with the stuffing and gravy.

Combining a medley of flavors, this aromatic stuffing features herbs, including sage, thyme, and parsley, and dried cranberries. It can be made a day ahead and then reheated with a little stock to moisten it before serving.

Mushroom Stuffing with Herbs and Cranberries

serves 10–12

3 tablespoons plus ½ cup
(5 ½ oz/170 g) unsalted butter

1 tablespoon olive oil

1 lb (500 g) assorted mushrooms such as cremini, shiitake, and portobello, brushed clean and sliced or coarsely chopped

2 teaspoons chopped fresh thyme

2 yellow onions, chopped

3 ribs celery, chopped

10–12 cups (1 ½ lb/750 g) unseasoned dried bread cubes

1 cup (4 oz/125 g) dried cranberries

⅓ cup (½ oz/15 g) chopped fresh flat-leaf (Italian) parsley

1 ½ tablespoons finely chopped fresh sage

3–4 cups (24–32 fl oz/750 ml–1 l) chicken stock

1–1 ½ teaspoons kosher salt

½ teaspoon freshly ground pepper

In a large frying pan over medium-high heat, melt the 3 tablespoons butter with the olive oil. Add the mushrooms and cook, stirring occasionally, until lightly browned, 6–8 minutes. Scrape into a large bowl and stir in the thyme until well blended. Set aside.

Preheat the oven to 350°F (180°C). Butter a 9-by-13-by-2-inch (23-by-33-by-5-cm) rimmed baking sheet.

Melt the remaining ½ cup (4 oz/125 g) butter in the same frying pan over medium heat. Add the onions and celery and cook, stirring frequently, until softened, 10–12 minutes. Remove from the heat and add to the mushrooms. Then add the bread cubes, cranberries, parsley, and sage and stir to mix. Gently stir in about 2 ½ cups (20 fl oz/625 ml) of the stock, or enough to moisten the mixture without making it wet. Add salt to taste and the pepper.

Transfer the mixture to the prepared pan and drizzle the surface evenly with about ½ cup (4 fl oz/125 ml) of the stock. Cover with aluminum foil. About 30 minutes before the turkey is done, place the stuffing in the oven and bake until heated through, about 30 minutes. Remove the foil and drizzle with some stock. Continue to bake, uncovered, until the surface is lightly browned and crispy, about 15 minutes longer. If the stuffing seems dry, moisten with a little more stock. Keep warm until serving time.

This delicious pan gravy calls for making a roux, a mixture of flour and a fat such as butter, to thicken it slightly. For more flavor, Calvados is added as a finishing touch, but Cognac or other brandies can be used in its place.

Cider-Shallot Pan Gravy

serves 10–12

6 tablespoons (3 oz/90 g)
unsalted butter

½ cup (3 oz/90 g) sliced shallots

2 tablespoons chopped fresh thyme
or 2 teaspoons dried thyme

6 tablespoons (2 oz/60 g) all-purpose
(plain) flour

Pan juices from Roast Turkey Seasoned
with Sage (page 158), optional

About 4 ½–5 cups (36–40 fl oz/1.1–1.25 l)
chicken stock

½ cup (4 fl oz/125 ml) apple cider

3 tablespoons Calvados or brandy

Salt and freshly ground pepper

prep tip

The thyme can be replaced with
a different herb, such as lemon thyme,
oregano, sage, or rosemary.

In a saucepan over medium-high heat, melt the butter. Add the shallots and thyme and sauté until the shallots are golden brown, about 8 minutes. Add the flour and cook, stirring frequently, until lightly browned, about 5 minutes.

Measure the pan juices, if using, and add enough stock to total 5 cups (40 fl oz/1.25 l). Gradually whisk the stock mixture into the butter mixture. Bring to a boil, whisking frequently. Mix in the cider and boil until lightly thickened, about 10 minutes. Add the Calvados and return the mixture to a boil. Season to taste with salt and pepper.

Pour into a warmed gravy boat and serve with the roast turkey.

Grilled Turkey with Maple Glaze

serves 8–10

1 turkey, 10–12 lb (5–6 kg)

10 qt (10 l) water

1 ½ cups (12 oz/375 g) kosher salt

1 cup (8 oz/250 g) sugar

4 bay leaves

10 black peppercorns

6 cloves garlic, crushed

3 handfuls of cherry, maple,
or mesquite wood chips

8 large fresh thyme sprigs

1 large yellow onion, quartered

1 Granny Smith apple or other tart
apple, quartered

2 tablespoons unsalted butter,
at room temperature

1 teaspoon *each* sea salt and freshly
ground pepper

Olive oil for brushing

MAPLE GLAZE

¼ cup (2 ¾ fl oz/75 ml)
pure maple syrup

2 tablespoons fresh lemon juice

2 cloves garlic, crushed

¼ cup (2 fl oz/60 ml) bourbon

2 tablespoons unsalted butter

About 1 hour before grilling, remove the turkey from the refrigerator. Remove the giblets and neck from the turkey cavity and reserve for another use. In a pot large enough to hold the turkey, combine the water, kosher salt, sugar, bay leaves, peppercorns, and garlic. Put the turkey in the brine. If it does not submerge, place a weight on it to hold it down. Refrigerate for at least 8 hours and up to 24 hours.

In a large bowl, soak the wood chips in water to cover for 20 minutes. Prepare a charcoal or gas grill for indirect grilling over medium heat. (For a charcoal grill, put a drip pan on the center of the grill grate and pile the coals on either side; for a gas grill, turn off half of the burners.)

Remove the turkey from the brine and pat dry. Put 6 of the thyme sprigs, the onion, and the apple in the cavity. Tie the legs together with wet kitchen string and fasten the loose neck skin with a metal skewer. Rub the outside of the turkey with the remaining 2 sprigs of thyme, then rub with the butter. Sprinkle with the salt and pepper.

Brush the grill rack with olive oil. Remove half of the wood chips from the water and scatter over the coals. If using a gas grill, put the chips in a smoker box, or in a heavy-duty foil packet with a few holes poked in it, and place on the lit burner(s). Cover the grill and heat until the chips start to smoke, about 10 minutes. Place the grill rack 4–6 inches (10–15 cm) from the fire. Place the turkey, breast side down, over the drip pan on the charcoal grill or over the unlit burner(s) on the gas grill. Re-cover and cook for 10–14 minutes per pound (500 g), adding more hot coals to the charcoal grill every 20–25 minutes to maintain the fire. After 1 hour, drain the remaining wood chips and scatter them over the coals, or put them in the smoker box or another foil packet and place on the lit burner(s).

Meanwhile, make the glaze. In a saucepan over medium heat, combine the maple syrup, lemon juice, garlic, bourbon, and butter and bring to a boil, stirring. Boil for 1 minute, then set aside.

serving tip

Leftover turkey, especially the breast meat, is perfect for sandwiches. For an afternoon or late-night snack, spread slices of baguette with leftover cranberry sauce and add turkey, arugula, and brie or Cheddar cheese.

After the turkey has been cooking for 1 ½ hours, brush with some of the maple glaze, warming it first, and replace the cover. Continue cooking until an instant-read thermometer inserted into the thickest part of a thigh away from the bone registers 170°–175°F (77°–80°C), about 2 ½ hours total.

Transfer the turkey to a carving board, tent with aluminum foil, and let rest for at least 30 minutes.

Carve the turkey (page 152), arrange on a warmed platter, and serve with Sausage, Apple, and Thyme Stuffing (recipe below).

Sausage, Apple, and Thyme Stuffing

serves 8–10

4 tablespoons (2 oz/60 g) unsalted butter

¼ lb (125 g) bulk pork sausage

½ cup (3 oz/90 g) minced yellow onion

3 ribs celery, minced

¼ cup (1 oz/30 g) coarsely chopped walnuts

1 Granny Smith apple, peeled, cored, and grated

3 slices dried apple, finely chopped

2 tablespoons fresh thyme leaves

6 slices day-old coarse country bread, about 1 inch (2.5 cm) thick, crusts removed and cut into cubes

1 teaspoon *each* sea salt and freshly ground pepper

½–1 cup (4–8 fl oz/125–250 fl ml) chicken stock

About 1 hour before the turkey is done, preheat the oven to 350°F (180°C). Lightly butter an 8-inch (20-cm) square baking dish.

In a large frying pan over medium-high heat, melt the butter. When it foams, crumble the sausage into the pan and cook, stirring, until opaque, about 3 minutes. Add the onion, celery, walnuts, grated apple, dried apple, thyme, bread, salt, and pepper. Stir in enough of the chicken stock to moisten the mixture without making it wet.

Transfer the stuffing to the prepared baking dish and cover tightly with aluminum foil. Bake until lightly browned, about 1 hour. Serve warm.

When you order your rack of lamb, ask the butcher to "french" it, or cut away the meat and tissue from the top 2 to 3 inches (5 to 7.5 cm) of each bone. This gives the chops a clean and attractive appearance that shows off the succulent meat.

Rack of Lamb with Garlic and Fresh Herbs

serves 8

1 ½ tablespoons sea salt

1 ½ tablespoons freshly ground pepper

1 tablespoon minced fresh thyme

1 tablespoon minced fresh sage

2 teaspoons minced fresh rosemary

3 racks of lamb, each 1 ½–1 ¾ lb (750–875 g) with 7 or 8 ribs, frenched

4 cloves garlic, peeled and cut lengthwise into thin slivers

⅓ cup (3 fl oz/80 ml) extra-virgin olive oil

½ cup (4 fl oz/125 ml) dry red wine

prep tip

Dry red wine varietals include Barolo, Burgundy, Cabernet Sauvignon, Merlot and Shiraz.

Preheat the oven to 400°F (200°C).

In a small bowl, combine the salt, pepper, thyme, sage, and rosemary and stir to mix well. Lightly pat the herb mixture over the fat side of the lamb. With the tip of a sharp knife, make a slit about 1 inch (2.5 cm) deep through the fat side and insert a garlic sliver into it. Repeat until all the slivers have been used, spacing the cuts about 2 inches (5 cm) apart.

Place 2 large, nonstick ovenproof frying pans over medium heat and divide the olive oil between them. When the oil is hot, add the 2 lamb racks to one pan and 1 rack to the other and sear on all sides until lightly golden, about 3 minutes per side. Carefully, pour off the fat from the frying pans, turn the lamb fat side up and place the frying pans in the oven. Roast until an instant-read thermometer inserted into the thickest part of the meat away from the bone registers 130°–140°F (54°–60°C) for medium-rare, 13–15 minutes; or 140°–150°F (60°–65°C) for medium, 15–20 minutes.

Transfer the lamb to a carving board and loosely tent with aluminum foil. Let rest for 10 minutes.

While the lamb is resting, return the frying pan that held the 2 racks to the stove top over medium-high heat. Add the wine and scrape the pan bottom to loosen the browned bits. Bring to a simmer and cook until the wine is reduced by half, about 2 minutes.

To serve, cut the racks apart into chops and divide them among warmed dinner plates. Spoon the pan juices over them and serve at once.

A whole baked ham is a welcome sight on nearly any holiday table; plus, it is easy to prepare. Carve the ham at the dining table and serve each guest, or set the sliced ham on a buffet and let guests serve themselves.

Baked Ham with Spiced Cider Glaze

serves 8–10

1 cup (8 fl oz/250 ml) apple cider

2 cinnamon sticks

20–25 whole cloves

3 star anise

1 fully cooked bone-in ham, about 8 lb (4 kg)

½ cup (3 ½ oz/105 g) firmly packed light brown sugar

¼ cup (3 fl oz/90 ml) honey

2 teaspoons dry mustard

Fresh herb sprigs for garnish

serving tip

If you have leftover ham, use it to make ham sandwiches on good-quality bread with your favorite mustard, or chop into small pieces and add to a frittata.

Preheat the oven to 325°F (165°C).

In a small saucepan over medium-high heat, combine the cider, the cinnamon sticks, 6 of the cloves, and the star anise. Bring to a boil, reduce the heat to low, cover, and simmer for 15 minutes. Remove from the heat. (The spiced cider can be made up to 24 hours ahead; cover and refrigerate until ready to use.)

Cut away and discard any skin on the ham, and trim the fat to ½ inch (12 mm) thick. Using a sharp knife, score the fat on the upper half of the ham in a diamond pattern, cutting about ¼ inch (6 mm) deep. Stick the remaining cloves at the corners of the diamonds. Line a shallow roasting pan with aluminum foil, and then put a rack in the pan. Place the ham, fat side up, on the rack. Bake for 1 ¼ hours.

In a small bowl, combine the brown sugar, honey, and mustard and mix well. Pat half of the sugar mixture over the scored surface of the ham. Stir the spiced cider into the remaining mixture. Continue to bake, basting several times with the cider mixture, until the ham is glazed and shining, about 1 hour longer.

Transfer the ham to a carving board and tent with aluminum foil. Let rest for 15 minutes. Carve the ham, arrange on a warmed platter, garnish with the herb sprigs, and serve.

Rosemary Rib Roast with Yorkshire Pudding

serves 8

4-rib standing rib roast,
about 8 lb (4 kg), tied

2 tablespoons unsalted butter,
at room temperature

3 tablespoons chopped fresh rosemary

Salt and freshly ground pepper

YORKSHIRE PUDDING

3 extra-large eggs

1 ½ cups (12 fl oz/375 ml) whole milk

1 ½ cups (7 ½ oz/235 g) all-purpose
(plain) flour

1 ¼ teaspoons kosher salt

Canola oil, if needed

2 cups (16 fl oz/500 ml) beef
or chicken stock

shopping tip

Look for a roast with a thick layer of white fat and marbling throughout the meat. Ask the butcher for the "first cut," which comes from the loin end and has the biggest eye, and to tie the roast to keep the fat from pulling away from the meat.

Remove the roast from the refrigerator about 1 hour before roasting. Position a rack in the lower third of the oven and preheat to 450°F (230°C). Rub the roast on all sides with the butter and rosemary. Season with salt and pepper.

To make the Yorkshire pudding batter, combine the eggs and milk in a blender and process just to combine. Add the flour and salt and process until smooth, about 30 seconds. Cover and refrigerate until needed.

Place the roast, rib bones down, in a roasting pan. Roast for 20 minutes. Reduce the heat to 350°F (180°C). Continue to roast until an instant-read thermometer inserted into the thickest part away from the bone registers 120°–130°F (52°–54°C) for rare to medium-rare, about 1 ¼–1 ¾ hours longer. Transfer to a carving board and loosely tent with aluminum foil. Let rest for 30 minutes. Position a rack in the upper third of the oven and raise the heat to 450°F (230°C).

Spoon the fat from the roasting pan into a small bowl. Add canola oil if needed to total ¼ cup (2 fl oz/60 ml) and reserve. Pour the stock into the roasting pan, place the pan on the stove top over low heat, and scrape the pan bottom to loosen the browned bits, stirring until dissolved. Pour the contents of the pan through a medium-mesh sieve into a measuring pitcher and reserve.

Put 1 teaspoon of the reserved fat in each of 12 nonstick standard muffin cups. Place in the oven to heat for 5 minutes. Pour 3–4 tablespoons of the batter into each hot muffin cup, filling them about two-thirds full. Return the pan to the oven and reduce the heat to 425°F (220°C). Bake until puffed and golden and a knife inserted into the center of 1 pudding comes out clean, about 30 minutes.

While the puddings are baking, prepare the *jus:* Pour the pan juices mixture into a saucepan, bring to a boil over high heat, and cook until reduced by one-third, about 5 minutes. Season with salt and pepper. Set aside and keep warm.

Remove the strings and cut along the rib bones to release the meat in a single large piece. Cut across the grain into thick slices. Serve with a little *jus* spooned over each slice. With the tip of a knife, lift each pudding from the muffin pan and serve with the roast.

Sides

Potato Gratin Rounds with Thyme **174**

Root Vegetable Purée **175**

Glazed Parsnips and Carrots with Sherry **177**

Mashed Potatoes and Celery Root **178**

Sautéed Fennel and Garlic **179**

Roasted Squash with Maple Syrup and Sage Cream **180**

Cauliflower Gratin **182**

Wild Rice with Mushrooms and Winter Squash **183**

Green Beans with Bacon and Onion Vinaigrette **185**

185 Broccoli Rabe with Lemon Zest

186 Brussels Sprouts with Shallots and Parmesan

187 Spicy Braised Escarole

188 Gingered Cranberries

188 Olive and Fennel Relish

191 Maple-Thyme Biscuits

192 Rosemary Popovers

193 Classic Dinner Rolls

194 Olive Bread

Everyone appreciates potatoes on the holiday table, and this is an especially elegant presentation, suitable to accompany any main dish. The potatoes are baked and then shaped into individual rounds with a biscuit cutter.

Potato Gratin Rounds with Thyme

serves 8

1 clove garlic, peeled and lightly crushed

5 tablespoons (2 ½ oz/75 g) unsalted butter

3 lb (1.5 kg) boiling potatoes such as Yukon gold, peeled, if desired

1 ½ yellow onions, thinly sliced

2 teaspoons sea salt

1 teaspoon freshly ground black pepper

½ teaspoon freshly grated nutmeg

⅓ lb (155 g) Gruyère cheese, shredded

1 ½ cups (12 fl oz/375 ml) whole milk

¼ cup (⅓ oz/10 g) minced fresh thyme

prep tip

Skip washing the potatoes after peeling. Washing removes starch, and the potatoes need the extra starch so the gratin will hold together better.

Photo on page 164

Preheat the oven to 425°F (220°C).

Rub an 8-by-12-by-2-inch (20-by-30-by-5-cm) baking dish with the garlic and grease heavily with 1 tablespoon of the butter. Cut the potatoes into slices ⅛ inch (3 mm) thick. Spread half of the potatoes and onions in the prepared baking dish. Sprinkle with half each of the salt, pepper, nutmeg, and cheese. Cut 3 tablespoons of the butter into small pieces and dot the top. Spread the remaining potatoes on top and sprinkle with the remaining salt, pepper, nutmeg, and cheese. Cut the remaining 1 tablespoon butter into small pieces and dot the top.

In a small saucepan over medium-high heat, bring the milk just to a boil. Pour the milk over the potatoes, carefully slipping a knife between the edge of the dish and the potatoes to help the milk run underneath.

Bake until the milk is absorbed, a golden brown crust forms, and the potatoes are easily pierced with a knife, 35–45 minutes.

Remove from the oven and let stand for 5 minutes. Cut the gratin into 8 equal rectangles. Using a spatula, lift each rectangle onto a work surface. Using a 2 ½- or 3-inch (6- or 7.5-cm) round biscuit cutter, cut each rectangle into a circle. (Reserve the scraps for leftovers). Place the rounds on individual plates or a serving platter, sprinkle with the thyme, and serve at once.

This purée can be made with any combination of root vergetables, which are fresh and delicious during the winter months. This side dish is a favorite addition to hearty roasts and stews.

Root Vegetable Purée

serves 6

1 large or 2 medium russet or Yukon gold potatoes, about 1 lb (500 g) total weight, peeled and cut into 1-inch (2.5-cm) chunks

2 lb (1 kg) root vegetables such as rutabagas, celery root (celeriac), parsnips, or carrots, or a combination, peeled and cut into 1-inch (2.5-cm) chunks

Salt

3 tablespoons vegetable oil

3 shallots, sliced into thin rounds

½ teaspoon sugar

4 tablespoons (2 oz/60 g) unsalted butter, cut into 4 equal pieces

Pinch of freshly grated nutmeg

Freshly ground pepper

Photo on page 149

In a saucepan over high heat, combine the potato, the root vegetables, 1 teaspoon salt, and water to cover by 1 inch (2.5 cm) and bring to a boil. Reduce the heat to medium and simmer rapidly, uncovered, until the vegetables are very tender when pierced with a knife, 20–30 minutes.

Meanwhile, in a frying pan over high heat, warm the oil. Separate the shallot slices into rings and add to the pan. Fry, stirring often, until golden brown, 4–7 minutes. Add the sugar and a generous pinch of salt and cook for 1 minute longer. The shallots should be crisp and well colored. Using a slotted spoon, transfer the shallots to paper towels to drain, arranging them in a single layer.

When the vegetables are tender, drain them, reserving 1 cup (8 fl oz/250 ml) of the cooking liquid. Return the vegetables to the saucepan and, using a potato masher or large wooden spoon, mash them, adding the butter pieces one at a time as you work. Add enough of the reserved cooking liquid to make a soft consistency. Season with the nutmeg and with salt and pepper to taste.

Transfer the purée to a warmed serving dish or bowl and sprinkle evenly with the shallots. Serve at once.

Parsnips, a root vegetable that has a shape and taste similar to carrots, are particularly delicious during cooler months, when the cold temperatures convert their starch to sugar, giving them their distinctive flavor.

Glazed Parsnips and Carrots with Sherry

serves 4

¾ lb (375 g) parsnips, peeled

½ lb (250 g) carrots, peeled

¾ cup (6 fl oz/180 ml) chicken stock or water

3 tablespoons unsalted butter

3 tablespoons dry sherry or Madeira

1 ½ teaspoons chopped fresh thyme or ½ teaspoon dried thyme

A few drops of fresh lemon juice

Salt and freshly ground pepper

prep tip

Dry types of sherry include fino and Manzanilla. Amontillado, considered a medium sherry, can also be used in this dish, as can any dry red wine.

Cut the parsnips and carrots in half lengthwise, and then cut the halves in half lengthwise again if they are very thick. If the pieces are large, cut them in half crosswise to make finger-length sticks. All of the pieces should be more or less the same thickness. If the cores are distinctly darker and denser than the rest of the root, remove them with a paring knife.

Arrange the parsnips and carrots in a single layer in a frying pan large enough to accommodate them without crowding. Add the chicken stock, butter, sherry, and thyme and season with salt. Toss gently to mix. Partially cover the pan and place over medium heat. Bring to a simmer and cook until the parsnips are easily pierced with a knife, 6–8 minutes.

Uncover the pan, raise the heat to high, and continue to cook, uncovered, until the juices are reduced to a glaze, 4–6 minutes. Season to taste with the lemon juice, salt, and pepper.

Transfer to a warmed serving dish and serve immediately.

This flavorful combination, prepared with plenty of butter and cream, makes a crowd-pleasing side dish for the holiday roast turkey or beef. Celery root tastes similar to celery but has a softer, denser texture and a mild lemony tang.

Mashed Potatoes and Celery Root

serves 6–8

1 lb (500 g) celery root (celeriac), peeled and cut into 1-inch (2.5-cm) cubes

1 ½ lb (750 g) Yukon gold potatoes, peeled and cut into 1-inch (2.5-cm) cubes

2 teaspoons sea salt

½ cup (4 fl oz/125 ml) heavy (double) cream

¼ cup (2 fl oz/60 ml) whole milk

3 tablespoons unsalted butter, at room temperature

1 teaspoon freshly ground pepper

shopping tip

Other potatoes, such as russets or Yellow Finns, can be used in place of the Yukon golds.

In a saucepan, combine the celery root and potatoes with water to cover by 2 inches (5 cm). Add 1 teaspoon of the salt and bring to a boil over high heat. Cover and reduce the heat to medium. Cook until the vegetables are very tender when pierced with a knife, 10–15 minutes.

Drain thoroughly in a colander and return to the warm saucepan. Add the cream, milk, butter, the remaining 1 teaspoon salt, and the pepper. Using a potato masher or an electric mixer, beat until smooth and creamy.

Transfer to a warmed serving bowl or platter and serve immediately.

Fennel is a popular vegetable on the holiday tables of Italy and France, where it is often eaten raw or sautéed, as it is prepared here. Its sweet aniselike flavor makes it a good accompaniment to almost any roasted meat or fish.

Sautéed Fennel and Garlic

serves 6–8

3 fennel bulbs, about 1 ½ lb
(750 g) total weight

3 tablespoons extra-virgin olive oil

2 tablespoons minced yellow onion

6 cloves garlic, halved

1 teaspoon salt

shopping tip

When selecting fennel, pick bulbs
that are firm and blemish free.

Cut off the stems and feathery fronds of the fennel bulb and remove any bruised or discolored outer layers. Cut the bulb in half lengthwise and cut out any tough core parts. Using a mandoline or a sharp knife, cut the bulb halves crosswise into slices about ¼ inch (6 mm) thick. Cut each slice lengthwise into 4 equal strips.

In a frying pan, warm the olive oil over medium-high heat. Add the onion and sauté until translucent, 2–3 minutes. Add the fennel, garlic, and salt and continue to sauté until the fennel takes on a sheen, about 5 minutes. Reduce the heat to low and cover the pan. Continue to cook until the fennel is very soft and tender, about 15 minutes. Transfer to a serving bowl and serve at once.

The maple syrup reflects the inherent sweetness of the roasted squash, while the sage-infused cream adds a savory element. This quintessential fall and winter dish is a classic accompaniment to roast turkey or baked ham.

Roasted Squash with Maple Syrup and Sage Cream

serves 8

2 acorn squashes, about 2 ½ lb (1.25 kg) total weight

2 tablespoons extra-virgin olive oil

1 ½ teaspoons sea salt

1 ½ teaspoons freshly ground pepper

1 cup (8 fl oz/250 ml) heavy (double) cream

8 large fresh sage sprigs, plus 2 teaspoons minced sage

Pure maple syrup for drizzling

prep tip

To add some crunch to the dish, roast the seeds from the squash and sprinkle on top of the finished dish just before serving.

Preheat the oven to 350°F (180°C).

Cut the squashes crosswise into rounds 1 inch (2.5 cm) thick. Using a spoon, scrape out the seeds and discard them. Brush the rounds on both sides with the olive oil, place on a baking sheet, and sprinkle them with the salt and pepper. Roast, turning once, until tender, 45–60 minutes.

Meanwhile, in a saucepan over low heat, combine the cream and sage sprigs and bring to a simmer. Cook, stirring occasionally, until the cream has thickened and is infused with the sage, about 30 minutes. Remove the sprigs and discard them. Add the minced sage, bring the cream to a boil, and cook until reduced to about ⅔ cup (5 fl oz/160 ml).

Transfer the squash to a platter. Drizzle with the maple syrup and a small amount of the sage cream and serve at once. Pass any remaining cream in a small pitcher at the table.

Green Beans with Bacon and Onion Vinaigrette

serves 8

4 slices bacon

3 tablespoons minced red onion

4 tablespoons (2 fl oz/60 ml) extra-virgin olive oil

1 ½ tablespoons red wine vinegar

½ teaspoon Dijon mustard

Sea salt and freshly ground pepper

2 lb (1 kg) green beans, stem and tip ends trimmed

In a frying pan over medium-high heat, fry the bacon until crisp, about 5 minutes. Transfer to paper towels to drain. Pour off all but 1 tablespoon of the fat, return the pan to medium heat, add the onion, and sauté until soft, 1–2 minutes. Transfer to a small bowl and stir in 2 tablespoons of the oil, the vinegar, the mustard, salt to taste, and 1 teaspoon pepper. Set aside.

Bring a large pot three-fourths full of water to a boil over high heat and stir in 2 teaspoons salt. Add the green beans, reduce the heat to medium-high, and cook until the beans are just tender, 5–7 minutes. Drain, rinse under cold water, and wrap in a kitchen towel to dry.

In a frying pan over medium-high heat, warm the remaining 2 tablespoons olive oil. When the oil is hot, add the beans and sauté until shiny and hot, 3–4 minutes. Remove from the heat and stir in the vinaigrette.

Transfer to a serving bowl or platter, break or crumble the bacon into large pieces on top, and serve hot.

Broccoli Rabe with Lemon Zest

serves 8

2 bunches broccoli rabe, about 4 lb (2 kg) total weight

1 lemon

2 tablespoons extra-virgin olive oil

2 cloves garlic, minced

½ teaspoon sea salt

Trim the coarse ends of the broccoli rabe and discard. Coarsely chop the rest into bite-sized pieces. Grate 2 teaspoons of the zest from the lemon. Halve the lemon and squeeze 1 tablespoon of the juice. Set the zest and juice aside.

In a large frying pan over medium-high heat, warm the olive oil. Add the garlic and cook just until golden, about 1 minute. Add the broccoli rabe and salt and sauté until tender to the bite, about 5 minutes. Add the lemon zest and juice and stir to coat the greens.

Transfer to a serving bowl or platter and serve hot.

Cutting Brussels sprouts lengthwise into thin slices gives them a festive appearance and interesting texture. Adding them to the same pan in which the shallots were caramelized captures extra flavor for the dish.

Brussels Sprouts with Shallots and Parmesan

serves 8

2 lb (1 kg) Brussels sprouts

1 tablespoon unsalted butter

3 tablespoons extra-virgin olive oil

4 shallots, thinly sliced

1 ½ teaspoons sea salt

⅔ cup (5 fl oz/160 ml) dry vermouth or dry white wine

½ cup (4 fl oz/125 ml) chicken stock

1 teaspoon freshly ground pepper

½ cup (2 oz/60 g) grated Parmesan cheese

prep tip

For added flavor and heartiness, add crumbled cooked pancetta or toasted nuts with the pepper.

Photo on page 170

Cut off any dry outer leaves from the Brussels sprouts. Trim away any brown bits, and slice off the dry stem end. Cut lengthwise into very thin slices.

Preheat the oven to 350°F (180°C).

In an ovenproof frying pan or sauté pan with a lid over medium-high heat, melt the butter with 1 tablespoon of the olive oil. When it foams, add the shallots and ¾ teaspoon of the salt and sauté just until the shallots begin to turn golden, about 3 minutes. Cover, reduce the heat to low, and cook, stirring occasionally, until the shallots are golden brown, about 10 minutes. Add 1 tablespoon of the olive oil, raise the heat to medium-high, and add the Brussels sprouts and the remaining ¾ teaspoon salt. Cook, stirring often, until the Brussels sprouts wilt, 2–3 minutes. Raise the heat to high, add the vermouth, and stock. Scrape the pan bottom to loosen the browned bits.

Cover the pan and place it in the oven. Cook until the Brussels sprouts are tender, about 7–10 minutes.

Remove from the oven and toss with the pepper and the remaining 1 tablespoon olive oil. Transfer to a serving dish and sprinkle with the Parmesan cheese. Serve hot.

The Italians cook escarole in a number of ways, including braised, which mellows its slight bitterness. Here, a sprinkle of red pepper flakes is added, giving the dish an extra bit of flavor that pairs well with both poultry and fish.

Spicy Braised Escarole

serves 8

2 tablespoons unsalted butter

2 cloves garlic, minced

3 tablespoons minced yellow onion

2 heads escarole (Batavian endive), tough outer leaves discarded and tender leaves coarsely chopped

2 teaspoons red pepper flakes

1 teaspoon salt

1 teaspoon freshly ground black pepper

¼ cup (2 fl oz/60 ml) dry vermouth

3 cups (24 fl oz/750 ml) chicken stock

Photo on page 149

In a large sauté or saucepan, melt the butter over medium-high heat. When it foams, add the garlic and onion and sauté until the onion is translucent, about 2 minutes. Add the escarole and sauté, turning often, until the escarole is glistening, about 2 minutes. Sprinkle with the red pepper flakes, salt, and pepper and sauté for 1–2 minutes longer. Stir in the vermouth, then add the chicken stock, cover, and reduce the heat to low.

Cook until the escarole is very soft and tender and most of the liquid has been absorbed, 15–20 minutes. If there is still quite a bit of liquid left, raise the heat to high and cook until it evaporates.

Transfer to a serving bowl and serve hot.

Gingered Cranberries

serves 6–8

2 cups (8 oz/250 g) fresh cranberries

2 cups (16 fl oz/500 ml) water

1 cup (8 oz/250 g) sugar

2 tablespoons candied ginger, minced,
plus extra for garnish

In a large saucepan over medium-high heat, combine the cranberries, water, and sugar and bring to a boil. Reduce the heat to medium and cook, stirring often, until the juices have thickened and a few berries have begun to pop, 10–15 minutes. Stir in the 2 tablespoons candied ginger, remove from the heat, and let cool to room temperature.

Transfer to a serving bowl and serve chilled or at room temperature with a few pieces of candied ginger on top.

Olive and Fennel Relish

serves 8

1 small fennel bulb

2 cups (10 oz/315 g) pitted black
Mediterranean-style olives,
finely chopped

1 tablespoon finely chopped shallot

1 teaspoon fennel seeds, coarsely
crushed in a mortar or spice grinder

1 teaspoon coriander seeds

2 teaspoons grated lemon zest

1 teaspoon fresh lemon juice

1–2 tablespoons extra-virgin olive oil

Salt (optional)

Cut off the stems and feathery fronds of the fennel bulb and remove any bruised or discolored outer layers. Cut the bulb in half lengthwise and cut out any tough core parts. Chop coarsely and transfer to a food processor or a blender. Pulse to chop finely, about 10 times.

Transfer the fennel to a large bowl. Add the olives, shallot, fennel seeds, coriander seeds, lemon zest and juice, and 1 tablespoon of the olive oil and stir to mix. Add more olive oil if needed to make a moist, but not runny, relish. Taste and add salt, if desired.

Serve at room temperature.

These baking-powder biscuits are simple to make. To ensure they don't turn out too dense, use a light hand with the mixing and kneading, working the ingredients just enough for the dough to hold together.

Maple-Thyme Biscuits

makes 12–14 biscuits

2 cups (10 oz/315 g) all-purpose (plain) flour

1 tablespoon baking powder

1 teaspoon salt

2 teaspoons minced fresh thyme

⅓ cup (3 oz/90 g) cold unsalted butter, cut into 1-inch (2.5-cm) chunks

¾ cup (6 fl oz/180 ml) whole milk

3 tablespoons pure maple syrup

serving tip

For added sweetness, serve these biscuits with a small pitcher of maple syrup to drizzle over the top.

Preheat the oven to 450°F (230°C). Have ready an ungreased baking sheet.

In a large bowl, whisk together the flour, baking powder, salt, and thyme. Add the butter chunks and, using a pastry blender or two knives, cut the butter into the flour mixture until the mixture is the size of peas. In a small bowl, stir together the milk and maple syrup and pour into the dough. Using a fork, mix just until the dry ingredients are moistened. Using your hands, gather the dough into a rough ball and knead a few times in the bowl.

On a lightly floured work surface, roll the dough out into a circle about ½ inch (12 mm) thick. Using a floured 2 ½-inch (6-cm) round biscuit cutter, cut out as many rounds as you can and place them on the baking sheet. Gather the dough scraps and roll again, then cut out more rounds. (These may not be as perfect as the first ones). Add to the baking sheet.

Bake until the tops are pale gold and the biscuits have puffed slightly, about 10 minutes. Serve at once.

A welcome accompaniment to the holiday table, popovers are a classic quick bread characterized by a crisp, brown exterior and a moist, almost-hollow center. Here, rosemary adds a touch of both fragrance and flavor.

Rosemary Popovers

makes 12 popovers

2 large eggs

¼ teaspoon salt

1 cup (8 fl oz/250 ml) whole milk

2 tablespoons unsalted butter, melted

1 cup (5 oz/155 g) all-purpose (plain) flour

2 teaspoons minced fresh rosemary leaves

prep tip

Other herbs, such as sage or thyme, can be added along with, or in place of, the rosemary.

Lightly butter a standard 12-cup muffin pan or a popover pan.

In a large bowl, whisk together the eggs and salt. Stir in the milk and butter. Using a wooden spoon, beat in the flour and rosemary just until blended, being careful not to overbeat. (It's fine if there are a few lumps in the batter.)

Fill each cup one-half to two-thirds full and place the pan in the cold oven. Set the oven temperature to 425°F (220°C) and bake for 20 minutes. Reduce the oven temperature to 375°F (190°C) and bake until the popovers are golden and crisp on the outside, 10–15 minutes longer.

Quickly pierce each popover with a thin metal skewer or the tip of a small knife to release the steam. Leave the popovers in the oven for a couple of minutes longer so they will crisp a bit more, and then serve at once.

Despite the name, these rolls are perfect anytime—wonderful for dipping in sauce at supper, for serving alongside a salad at midday, or for spreading with jam first thing in the morning. These rolls are best served warm right from the oven.

Classic Dinner Rolls

makes 16 rolls

1 package (2 ½ teaspoons) active dry yeast

¼ cup (2 fl oz/60 ml) warm water (105°–115°F/40°–46°C)

1 cup (8 fl oz/250 ml) whole milk

2 tablespoons sugar

2 large eggs, at room temperature, plus 1 large egg, beaten

6 tablespoons (3 oz/90 g) unsalted butter, at room temperature

4 ½ cups (22 ½ oz/705 g) all-purpose (plain) flour, plus extra for kneading

2 teaspoons salt

To make by hand: In a large bowl, dissolve the yeast in the warm water and let stand until foamy, about 5 minutes. Using a whisk, beat in the milk, sugar, 2 eggs, butter, 4 ½ cups flour, and salt just until mixed, then stir with a wooden spoon until a rough mass forms. Scrape onto a floured work surface. Knead until smooth and elastic, dusting the work surface with flour to keep the dough from sticking, 5–7 minutes. The dough should be soft but not sticky.

To make in a stand mixer: In the bowl of a stand mixer, dissolve the yeast in the warm water and let stand until foamy, about 5 minutes. Add the milk, sugar, 2 eggs, butter, 4 ½ cups flour, and salt. Place the bowl on the mixer, attach the dough hook, and knead on low speed. Add a little more flour if the dough is sticking to the sides of the bowl after a few minutes of kneading. Knead until smooth, 5–7 minutes. The dough should be soft but not sticky.

Form the dough into a ball, transfer to a lightly oiled bowl, and cover with plastic wrap. Let rise in a warm spot until doubled in bulk, 1 ½–2 hours.

Line a large baking sheet with parchment (baking) paper. Punch down the dough and turn it out onto a lightly floured work surface. Cut it in half with a sharp knife, and then cut each half into 8 equal pieces. Roll each piece against the work surface into a round ball. Place the balls on the prepared pan, spacing them evenly, and cover with a kitchen towel. Let rise until puffy and soft when gently squeezed, 30–40 minutes. Position a rack in the lower third of the oven and preheat to 400°F (200°C).

Brush the rolls lightly with the beaten egg and bake until puffed and golden brown, 20–25 minutes. Serve at once.

Flavorful olives stud this bread, making it moist and rich tasting. It is a great accompaniment to a simple green salad. You can change the character of the loaf by using different types of olives, such as Gaeta, or a mix of varieties.

Olive Bread

makes 2 round loaves

3 packages (7 ½ teaspoons)
active dry yeast

2 cups (16 fl oz/500 ml) warm water
(105°–115°F/40°–46°C)

²/₃ cup (5 fl oz/160 ml)
extra-virgin olive oil

2 cups (10 oz/315 g) bread flour

4 cups (1 ¼ lb/625 g) all-purpose (plain)
flour, plus extra for kneading and
dusting the loaves

1 tablespoon sea salt

2 cups (10 oz/315 g) Kalamata olives,
pitted and coarsely chopped

In the bowl of a stand mixer, dissolve the yeast in the warm water and let stand until foamy, about 5 minutes. Add the olive oil, the bread flour and the 4 cups all-purpose flour, and the salt. Attach the bowl on the mixer, attach the dough hook, and knead on low speed. Add a little flour as needed for the dough to come away from the sides of the bowl after a few minutes. Knead until the dough is smooth and elastic, 5–7 minutes. Transfer the dough to a floured work surface, sprinkle the olives over the top, and knead them briefly and gently into the dough. Form the dough into a ball, place in a lightly oiled bowl, cover the bowl with a damp kitchen towel, and let rise in a warm spot until doubled in bulk, 1–1 ½ hours.

Punch down the dough and turn it out onto a lightly floured work surface. Knead it briefly and gently to disperse the olives evenly. Using a sharp knife, cut the dough in half. Cover with a kitchen towel and let rest for 5 minutes. Line a large baking sheet with parchment (baking) paper. Shape each half into a tight round on the work surface, rotating it in a circular motion between your palms. Put the loaves on the prepared pan, spacing them generously apart. Cover with a kitchen towel and let rise in a warm spot until doubled in bulk, 30–40 minutes. Position a rack in the lower third of the oven and preheat to 450°F (230°C).

Dust the tops of the loaves with flour. Using a serrated knife, slash a half crescent the length of each loaf, just off-center. Place in the oven, reduce the heat to 425°F (220°C), and bake until the loaves are golden brown and sound hollow when tapped on the bottom, 35–40 minutes. Let cool on wire racks.

Desserts

Serving Cheese **198**

Poached Pears in Red Wine **201**

Cardamom Crème Brûlée **202**

Macadamia-Caramel Tart **203**

Chocolate Pots de Crème **204**

Almond Pound Cake with Cherry Glaze **206**

Crème Anglaise **207**

Cinnamon-Spiced Whipped Cream **207**

Latticed Apple Pie **209**

Pumpkin Pie with Walnut Crust **210**

Seasonal Pie Toppings **213**

214 Persimmon Bread Pudding

215 Gingerbread Bundt Cake

217 Chocolate-Pecan Crostata

218 Pumpkin-Ginger Cheesecake

220 Cranberry and Pear Crisp

221 Rich Chocolate Brownie Cake

222 Ideas for Decorating Cakes

224 Apple Tarte Tatin

225 Cinnamon Ice Cream

227 Blood Orange Granita

228 Ice Cream Truffles

winter cheese plate

BANON

(goat's milk)

BLEU D'AUVERGNE OR STILTON

(cow's milk, blue veined)

CROTTIN DE CHAVIGNOL OR VALENÇAY

(goat's milk, creamy)

serve with *dried cranberries, pears,*
walnuts; Pouilly-Fumé, Sauvignon Blanc

italian cheese plate

GORGONZOLA

(cow's milk, blue veined)

PECORINO SARDO OR ROMANO

(sheep's milk, hard)

TALEGGIO OR CRESCENZA

(cow's milk, soft)

serve with *salami, olives, crostini;*
Prosecco, Lambrusco, Chianti, Sangiovese

artisanal cheese plate

ENGLISH FARMHOUSE CHEDDAR

(cow's milk, hard)

VALENÇAY OR HUMBOLDT FOG

(goat's milk, soft)

RED HAWK

(cow's milk, soft, triple cream)

serve with *cheese straws (page 94)*
or gougères, dates, toasted almonds;
Sauternes, Viognier, Pinot Noir, port

Serving Cheese

A composed cheese plate makes a memorable ending to a holiday meal—a chance to prolong the pleasures of wine and conversation before dessert. It can also be an easy appetizer or the main offering at a casual get-together.

selecting the cheeses

A well-balanced cheese platter should include a variety of tastes and textures. Choose some fresh and some aged cheeses, and vary the kinds of milk they are made from, such as a cow's milk Cheddar or Morbier, a goat's milk *crottin*, and a sheep's milk pecorino. You may want to include a blue, like Gorgonzola or Stilton, as well as a double or triple cream, like Brie or St. André. And don't overlook American artisanal cheeses, such as northern California's Red Hawk or Vermont's Cabot Cheddar.

putting it together

Arrange the cheeses on a cutting board or platter and include a spreader for each soft cheese and a sharp paring knife or cheese plane for hard cheeses. You can round out the presentation with thinly sliced fresh fruit, such as apples or pears; dried fruits, including figs, apricots, and cranberries; and toasted nuts, such as almonds, walnuts, and pecans. Jams, fruit preserves, chutneys, honey, and fig or quince paste all make excellent accompaniments.

finishing touches

At Thanksgiving, decorate the platter with grape or olive leaves. For Christmas or New Year's, add a festive garnish, such as tiny red flowers or ornaments and green foliage, or an artfully curled silver or gold ribbon. Offer a bread basket or board with baguette rounds and thin slices of dark bread, such as walnut bread. Before dinner, accompany cheese with sparkling wine or aperitifs. When serving a cheese course, you can keep pouring the red wine you served with the main course, or you can switch to a crisp white, rosé, sparkling wine, sherry, port, or dessert wine.

Fruity Pinot Noir, along with a vanilla bean and colorful raspberry purée, updates this classic pear dessert. Seckel pears, with their smooth, slightly granular flesh are a good variety to use. Winter Nellis or Bosc are also good pears for poaching.

Poached Pears in Red Wine

serves 4

4 firm but ripe Seckel pears, peeled with stems intact

2 ½ cups (20 fl oz/625 ml) Pinot Noir or other light, fruity red wine

½ cup (4 oz/125 g) sugar

1 lemon zest strip, 2 inches (5 cm) long by ¾ inch (2 cm) wide

2-inch (5-cm) piece vanilla bean

1 ½ cups (12 fl oz/375 ml) water

1 cup (4 oz/125 g) fresh or thawed frozen unsweetened raspberries

½ cup (2 oz/60 g) fresh raspberries

serving tip

Pass thin wafers of bittersweet chocolate to accompany the ruby pears.

Place the pears in a nonaluminum saucepan large enough to hold them lying down. Add the wine, sugar, lemon zest, vanilla bean, and the water.

Place the pan over medium-high heat and bring to a boil. Reduce the heat to medium-low, set a heatproof plate on top of the pears to keep them submerged in the liquid, and simmer gently until a thin knife inserted into the widest part of a pear pierces easily to the center, 35–40 minutes. Remove the plate covering the pears. Let the pears cool to room temperature in the liquid.

Meanwhile, make a raspberry purée. In a food processor or blender, purée the 1 cup (4 oz/125 g) fresh or frozen berries until smooth. Pass the purée through a fine-mesh sieve held over a bowl, pressing with the back of a wooden spoon to push as much of the purée through the sieve as possible. Discard the contents of the sieve. Set the purée aside.

Using a slotted spoon, lift the pears from the liquid. Set each pear in a shallow individual bowl, or place all 4 pears on a deep platter. Remove the zest and vanilla bean and discard or save the vanilla bean to garnish, if you like. Drizzle the raspberry purée onto the plate and garnish with a few fresh raspberries. Serve at room temperature.

The exotic flavors of cardamom and vanilla infuse these simple custards, which are best prepared 1 day in advance of serving. Thoroughly chill the custards before sprinkling them with sugar and caramelizing the tops.

Cardamom Crème Brûlée

serves 8

4 cups (32 fl oz/1 l) heavy (double) cream

2 vanilla beans, split lengthwise

4 pods white cardamom, cracked open

8 large egg yolks

1 ¼ cups (9 oz/280 g) superfine (caster) sugar

⅛ teaspoon salt

prep tip

If you own a kitchen torch, use it instead of the broiler to caramelize the sugar. The top of each custard should be a dark caramel color and brittle, while the custard itself should remain creamy.

Preheat the oven to 325°F (165°C). Select a baking dish 2–2 ½ inches (5–6 cm) deep and large enough to hold eight ¾-cup (6-fl oz/180-ml) ramekins. Line the dish with a kitchen towel.

In a large saucepan over medium heat, combine the cream, vanilla beans, and cardamom pods and their seeds. Bring to a simmer and cook for 1 minute. Remove the vanilla beans and, using the tip of a knife, scrape the seeds into the cream. Continue to simmer the cream for another 3–4 minutes, stirring. Remove from the heat and set aside.

In a large bowl, whisk together the egg yolks, ¾ cup (5 ½ oz/170 g) of the sugar, and the salt until thickened, about 2 minutes. Slowly add the warm, not hot, cream mixture, whisking constantly. Pour the custard through a fine-mesh sieve into a 1-qt (1-l) measuring pitcher. Skim off any bubbles from the surface. Divide the custard evenly among the prepared ramekins. Place the ramekins in the towel-lined dish and pour hot water into the dish to reach halfway up the sides of the ramekins. Cover loosely with aluminum foil.

Bake the custards until they are set but jiggle slighty when shaken, 20–25 minutes. Transfer the baking dish to a wire rack, let the custards cool slightly, and then lift the ramekins out of the water bath and set on the rack to cool for 1 hour. Cover tightly and refrigerate for at least 3 hours and up to overnight.

When just about ready to serve, preheat the broiler (grill). Sprinkle the top of each ramekin with 1 tablespoon of the remaining sugar. Place the custards on a baking sheet and place under the broiler about 4 inches (10 cm) from the heat source. Broil until the sugar caramelizes, 1–2 minutes.

A rich and slightly gooey nut tart makes an ideal dessert for a holiday buffet. This one can be made 1 day ahead and kept covered in a dry, cool place. Other nuts, such as pecans, or a mixture of nuts can be used in place of the macadamias.

Macadamia-Caramel Tart

serves 8

PASTRY

1 ¼ cups (6 ½ oz/200 g)
all-purpose flour

2 tablespoons sugar

¼ teaspoon salt

10 tablespoons (5 oz/155 g) cold
unsalted butter, cut into pieces

1 teaspoon vanilla extract (essence)

FILLING

1 cup (6 oz/185 g) coarsely chopped
salted macadamia nuts

⅔ cup (5 oz/155 g) sugar

3 tablespoons water

1 tablespoon light corn syrup

⅓ cup (3 fl oz/80 ml) heavy
(double) cream

1 tablespoon dark rum or 1 teaspoon
vanilla extract (essence)

To make the pastry, in a food processor, combine the flour, sugar, and salt and pulse once or twice to blend. Add the butter and vanilla and process until a smooth dough forms. Using your fingertips, gently press the dough evenly onto the bottom and up the sides of a 9-inch (23-cm) round tart pan with a removable bottom. Use your fingers to "cut" away any overhang. Freeze until firm, about 15 minutes. Preheat the oven to 375°F (190°C).

Place the pan on a baking sheet and prick the dough several times with a fork. Bake until the pastry is golden and cooked through, about 20 minutes. Let cool on a wire rack. Reduce the oven temperature to 325° F (165°C).

To make the filling, spread the nuts in a shallow pan and bake, stirring once or twice, until very lightly browned, 7–10 minutes. Pour onto a plate.

In a heavy saucepan over low heat, combine the sugar, water, and corn syrup. Cook, stirring occasionally, until the sugar dissolves, 1–2 minutes, then immediately wash down the sides of the pan with a pastry brush dipped in water. Increase the heat to medium-high, bring to a boil, and boil without stirring until the sugar turns a dark amber, 3–4 minutes. Swirl the pan frequently so the mixture cooks evenly. Remove from the heat and add the cream all at once (the mixture will bubble up vigorously), stirring to blend. Set aside for 8–10 minutes to thicken slightly.

Stir the nuts and rum into the warm caramel. Working quickly, spread the mixture evenly in the baked tart shell. Let cool until the filling is set, at least 15 minutes. Remove the pan sides and cut into wedges.

These elegant chocolate desserts go together quickly. It is important to bake them in a water bath to ensure they have a delicate, puddinglike texture. Be sure to allow at least 2 hours for them to set up in the refrigerator before serving.

Chocolate Pots de Crème

serves 6–8

1 cup (8 fl oz/250 ml) heavy (double) cream

1 ½ cups (12 fl oz/375 ml) whole milk

6 oz (185 g) bittersweet or semisweet (plain) chocolate, finely chopped

6 large egg yolks

¼ cup (2 oz/60 g) sugar

1 teaspoon vanilla extract (essence) or 2 tablespoons Grand Marnier or framboise

Cinnamon-Spiced Whipped Cream (page 207) for serving (optional)

Chocolate shavings for garnish (optional)

serving tip

Other possible garnishes include bits of candied citrus peel, candied violets, and fresh raspberries.

Position a rack in the middle of the oven and preheat to 300°F (150°C). Butter eight ½-cup (4-fl oz/125-ml) ramekins. Select a shallow baking dish large enough to hold the ramekins and line it with a kitchen towel.

In a saucepan over low heat, combine the cream, milk, and chocolate. Heat, whisking constantly, until the chocolate melts and the liquid is warm. Do not allow the mixture to boil. Remove from the heat.

In a bowl, whisk together the egg yolks and sugar until blended. While whisking constantly, slowly pour in the hot chocolate mixture until it is blended and the sugar dissolves. Stir in the vanilla. Pour the custard through a fine-mesh sieve into a 1-qt (1-l) measuring pitcher. Skim off any bubbles from the surface. Divide the custard evenly among the prepared ramekins. Pick up each ramekin and gently tap it on the counter a few times to remove any air bubbles. Place the ramekins in the towel-lined pan and pour hot water into the pan to reach halfway up the sides. Cover the pan with aluminum foil.

Bake the custards until they are set but still jiggle slightly when shaken, 30–40 minutes. Transfer the baking pan to a wire rack, let the custards cool slightly, and then lift the ramekins out of the water bath. Cover and refrigerate until well chilled, at least 2 hours and up to overnight.

Serve the custards topped with the whipped cream and chocolate shavings.

Pound cakes are traditionally made in loaf pans, which cause them to develop a mounded top as they bake. But pound cakes made in a tube pan come out perfectly level on top. Both the cake and cherry glaze can be made the day before serving.

Almond Pound Cake with Cherry Glaze

serves 8–10

2 ½ cups (7 ½ oz/235 g) sifted cake (soft-wheat) flour

½ teaspoon baking powder

½ teaspoon baking soda (bicarbonate of soda)

¼ teaspoon salt

1 ¼ cups (10 oz/315 g) unsalted butter, at room temperature

2 cups (16 oz/500 g) sugar

6 large eggs

¾ cup (6 fl oz/180 ml) buttermilk

1 ½ teaspoons almond extract (essence)

CHERRY GLAZE

1 cup (4 oz/125 g) dried cherries

1 cup (8 fl oz/250 ml) port wine

2 tablespoons sugar

1 jar (8 oz/250 g) cherry preserves

Preheat the oven to 350°F (180°C). Butter a 10-by-4-inch (25-by-10-cm) tube pan. Dust lightly with flour and shake out any excess.

In a large bowl, stir together the flour, baking powder, baking soda, and salt to mix well. In another large bowl, combine the butter and sugar and, using an electric mixer, beat until creamy and fluffy, about 2 minutes. Add the eggs one at a time, beating thoroughly after each addition.

Add the flour mixture to the egg mixture, one-third at a time, alternating with one-third of the buttermilk and beating thoroughly after each addition. Finally, beat in the almond extract. Pour the batter into the prepared pan, tapping the pan gently to release any air bubbles. Bake until the top is golden brown and a toothpick inserted into the center comes out nearly clean, 50–55 minutes.

Transfer to a wire rack and let cool in the pan for 15 minutes, then turn out of the pan, slipping a knife between edges of the cake and the pan to loosen any stuck edges. Turn the cake right side up and let cool while you make the glaze. (If making ahead, cover loosely and store in a cool, dry place.)

To make the glaze, in a small saucepan over medium-high heat, combine the dried cherries, port, and sugar and bring to a boil. Cook, stirring often, until the sugar dissolves. Stir in the preserves, reduce the heat to low, and simmer until thickened, 6–7 minutes. (If making ahead, let cool, cover, and store in the refrigerator. Reheat with 1–2 tablespoons water.)

To serve, drizzle the cake with the cherry glaze. Cut into slices and place on dessert plates. If desired, spoon warm Crème Anglaise (see next page) around the base and serve at once.

Here are two classic dessert garnishes, a classic French custard sauce and a delicious cinnamon-based whipped cream. They are both perfect for dressing up cake or pie slices or fruit desserts during the holidays.

Crème Anglaise

serves 8–10

2 cups (16 fl oz/500 ml) whole milk

2 large whole eggs plus 2 large egg yolks

¼ cup (2 oz/60 g) sugar

⅛ teaspoon salt

½ vanilla bean, split lengthwise

In the top of a double boiler set over (but not touching) simmering water, heat the milk to just below boiling, about 5 minutes. In a bowl, beat together the whole eggs and egg yolks just until blended. Beat in the sugar, salt, and vanilla bean, and then gradually stir in the hot milk. Return the mixture to the double boiler and raise the heat to bring the water to a boil. Cook over boiling water, stirring constantly, until thick enough to coat the back of a wooden spoon, 4–5 minutes. Remove from the heat and let cool slightly to thicken. Remove the vanilla bean and drizzle on top of the dessert of your choice.

Cinnamon-Spiced Whipped Cream

serves 8–10

1 cup (8 fl oz/250 ml) heavy (double) cream

¼ cup (1 oz/30 g) confectioners' (icing) sugar

1 teaspoon ground cinnamon

In a large bowl, using an electric mixer, whip the cream until soft peaks form, about 5 minutes. Add the confectioners' sugar and cinnamon and beat until stiff peaks form, 2–3 minutes longer. Cover and refrigerate until ready to use. Spoon a dollop of the cream on top of or alongside the dessert of your choice.

Latticed Apple Pie

PASTRY

2 cups (10 oz/315 g) all-purpose
(plain) flour

½ teaspoon salt

1 cup (8 oz/250 g) cold unsalted butter,
cut into 1-inch (2.5-cm) chunks

½ cup (4 fl oz/125 ml) ice water

FILLING

8 large tart baking apples, peeled,
halved, cored, and cut lengthwise into
slices ¼ inch (6 mm) thick

3 tablespoons all-purpose (plain) flour

¾ cup (6 oz/185 g) sugar

1 teaspoon ground cinnamon

½ teaspoon freshly grated nutmeg

1 tablespoon unsalted butter,
cut into small pieces

1 egg, lightly beaten

1 tablespoon sugar

prep tip

To make the lattice top shown here, use
a lattice cutter: press the rolled-out
dough between two plastic grids,
carefully remove it from the
grids, and place on the pie.

To make the pastry, in a bowl, whisk together the flour and the salt. Add the butter chunks and, using a pastry blender, cut the butter into the flour until the mixture is the size of small peas. Add the ice water and quickly work it in with your fingertips, gathering the dough into a ball. Divide the pastry in half and gently pat each half into a disk, wrap separately, and refrigerate.

On a lightly floured work surface, roll out 1 dough disk into a round about 13 inches (33 cm) in diameter and a scant ¼ inch (6 mm) thick. Lay the dough round in a 9-inch (23-cm) pie dish, gently patting it into the bottom and up the sides. Trim and crimp the edges. Set aside.

Preheat the oven to 425°F (220°C). Line a baking sheet with 2 pieces of aluminum foil.

To make the filling, put the apple slices in a large bowl. In a small bowl, stir together the flour, sugar, cinnamon, and nutmeg and sprinkle the mixture over the apples. Using your hands, turn to coat. Pile the apple mixture into the pie shell, mounding it in the center. Dot it with the butter.

To make the lattice without a lattice cutter: On a lightly floured work surface, roll the remaining dough disk into a circle about 13 inches (33 cm) in diameter and a scant ¼ inch (6 mm) thick. Using a sharp knife, cut it into strips about ¾ inch (2 cm) wide. Lay long strips vertically across the pie about ¾ inch (2 cm) apart. Starting at the top, weave a strip across horizontally. Do not trim the ends. Repeat until the pie is covered with the latticework. Crimp the ends of the latticework to match the edges of the bottom crust. Trim any excess pieces and use them to patch, if needed. Using a pastry brush, carefully brush the latticework with the beaten egg. Sprinkle the latticework with the sugar.

Place the pie on the prepared baking sheet. Fold up the top piece of aluminum foil, crimping the edges of the foil over the edges of the crust to prevent burning. Bake for 20 minutes. Tent the surface of the pie with another piece of foil. Continue baking at 425°F (220°C) for 10 minutes longer, then reduce the temperature to 400°F (200°C) and continue baking until the apples are tender and the crust is golden, 45–50 minutes longer. Transfer to a wire rack to cool.

Pumpkin Pie with Walnut Crust

serves 8

PASTRY

1 ¼ cups (6 ½ oz/200 g) all-purpose (plain) flour

½ cup (2 oz/60 g) coarsely ground walnuts

2 tablespoons confectioners' (icing) sugar

¼ teaspoon salt

½ cup (4 oz/125 g) cold unsalted butter, cut into small pieces

2 tablespoons ice water

FILLING

1 ¾ cups (14 oz/440 g) pumpkin purée

¾ cup (6 oz/185 g) granulated sugar

½ teaspoon salt

1 teaspoon ground cinnamon

½ teaspoon ground ginger

½ teaspoon freshly grated nutmeg

¼ teaspoon ground cloves

2 large eggs

1 cup (8 fl oz/250 ml) evaporated milk

½ cup (4 fl oz/125 ml) water

serving tip

Serve the pie with a dollop of whipped cream or a scoop of ice cream.

To make the pastry, in a food processor, combine the flour, walnuts, confectioners' sugar, and salt and pulse once or twice to blend. Add the butter pieces and pulse or process until the mixture is the size of small peas, about 45 seconds. With the machine running, add the ice water until the dough comes roughly together, adding up to 2 more teaspoons water if needed. Gather the dough into a ball and place it on a sheet of plastic wrap. Top with another piece of plastic wrap and flatten into a disk. Refrigerate overnight.

Bring the dough to room temperature 30–45 minutes before rolling. Pinch off a piece the size of a golf ball and set aside for the cutouts. On a lightly floured work surface, roll out the disk into a round 12 inches (30 cm) in diameter and about ¹⁄₁₆ inch (2 mm) thick. Lay the dough round in a 9-inch (23-cm) pie pan, gently patting it into the bottom and up the sides. Trim and crimp the edges.

Preheat the oven to 450°F (230°C).

To make the filling, in a large saucepan over medium heat, cook the pumpkin purée, stirring, until it begins to caramelize, about 5 minutes. Remove from the heat and stir in the granulated sugar, salt, cinnamon, ginger, nutmeg, and cloves. In a bowl, whisk together the eggs, milk, and water. Whisk the egg mixture into the pumpkin mixture.

Pour the filling into the pie shell. Roll out the reserved pastry on a lightly floured work surface. Cut out desired shapes and put them on a small prepared baking sheet as directed on page 213.

Bake the pie for 15 minutes. Reduce the oven temperature to 300°F (150°C), place the cutouts in the oven along with the pie, and bake the cutouts until golden brown, about 10 minutes. Remove the cutouts, transfer to a wire rack to cool, and continue to bake the pie until just the center jiggles when the pan is gently shaken, about 30 minutes longer. Transfer to a wire rack and let cool for at least 20 minutes.

Arrange the cutouts on the pie in an attractive pattern. Serve the pie warm or at room temperature, cut into wedges.

Seasonal Pie Toppings

A good way to spruce up a pie is to use leftover pastry dough to cut out small, festive shapes. The cutouts are baked separately and then placed on top of the baked pie. The hardest part is selecting your favorite cookie cutters.

making dough cutouts

Preheat the oven to 350°F (180°C). Line a baking sheet with parchment (baking) paper or silicone liner.

Place a chilled dough disk or pastry scraps (if using scraps, shape into a disk and refrigerate for a few minutes if the dough is warm and sticky) on a floured work surface. Using a lightly floured rolling pin, roll out into a circle about 1/16 inch (2 mm) thick.

Using small cookie cutters of your choice, cut out as many shapes as you like. Use a metal spatula to transfer the cutouts to the prepared baking sheet, spacing them 1 inch (2.5 cm) apart. Brush the top of each cutout with egg wash made by whisking together 1 egg with 1 tablespoon of water.

Bake the cutouts until golden brown, 10–15 minutes. Transfer to a wire rack and let cool. Arrange in an attractive pattern on top of a pie.

choosing seasonal cutouts

apple leaf Other types of leaf cookie cutters, such as maple or oak, can also be used. Use the tip of a sharp knife or a toothpick to make leaf vein marks. Place the leaves in a circle in the middle of a pie or near the crust.

holly and berries Place holly leaves and berries in the center of a pie, or arrange in a circle around the edge of the pie.

christmas tree Christmas tree cutouts come in different shapes and sizes. Mix them up to create a festive holiday pattern on top of a pie.

holiday star Stars add a fun element to any pie. Cut out different sizes and place in clusters in the center or all over the top of a pie.

apple leaf

holly and berries

christmas tree

holiday star

The texture of this dessert depends on the type of bread you use. Coarse-crumbed bread will easily absorb the egg mixture, resulting in a particularly fluffy pudding. Fine-crumbed bread will yield a more dense, though equally delicious, result.

Persimmon Bread Pudding

serves 6

4–6 cups (32–48 fl oz/1–1.5 l) whole milk

1 teaspoon vanilla extract (essence)

3 large eggs, lightly beaten

½ teaspoon freshly grated nutmeg

½ teaspoon ground cloves

1 ½ cups (12 oz/375 g) sugar

½ teaspoon salt

10–12 slices day-old bread, each about 1 inch (2.5 cm) thick, crusts removed

1 cup (8 oz/250 g) persimmon purée

2 tablespoons unsalted butter, at room temperature

prep tip

For an easy alternative, substitute canned pumpkin purée for the persimmon purée.

Preheat the oven to 350°F (180°C). Lightly butter a 9-by-5-inch (23-by-13-cm) loaf pan or other baking dish.

Pour 4 cups of the milk into a large bowl, if you are using a fine-textured or moist bread, and 5–6 cups (40–48 fl oz/1.25–1.5 l) if you are using a coarse, dry bread. Add the vanilla, eggs, nutmeg, cloves, ¾ cup (6 oz/185 g) of the sugar, and the salt and mix well. Add the bread and let stand just until the bread is thoroughly softened. It should not be soggy. Transfer to another bowl.

Arrange a layer of soaked bread in the prepared pan. Top with one-third of the persimmon purée. Pour about one-fourth of the egg mixture over the top. Repeat twice, pushing down the layers of bread as you go. Finish with a bread layer and pour over the remaining egg mixture.

In a large bowl, combine the butter and remaining ¾ cup sugar. Using your fingertips or a wooden spoon, crumble them together and sprinkle evenly over the top of the last bread layer.

Bake until a toothpick inserted into the center of the pudding comes out clean, 45–60 minutes. Transfer to a wire rack and let cool before serving.

To serve, scoop into bowls.

Gingerbread Bundt Cake

serves 12–16

3 cups (15 oz/470 g) all-purpose (plain) flour

½ teaspoon salt

1 teaspoon baking soda (bicarbonate of soda)

1 teaspoon *each* ground cinnamon and allspice

2 tablespoons ground ginger

¼ cup (1½ oz/45 g) peeled and grated fresh ginger

1 cup (8 oz/250 g) unsalted butter, at room temperature

1 cup (7 oz/220 g) firmly packed light brown sugar

1 large egg

1 cup (11 oz/345 g) light molasses

1 cup (8 fl oz/250 ml) buttermilk

NUTMEG WHIPPED CREAM (OPTIONAL)

1½ cups (12 fl oz/375 ml) heavy (double) cream

6 tablespoons (1½ oz/45 g) confectioners' (icing) sugar

1 tablespoon freshly grated nutmeg, plus extra for garnish

Preheat the oven to 350°F (180°C). Butter a 10-inch (25-cm) Bundt pan, including the tube. Dust lightly with flour and shake out any excess.

In a large bowl, whisk together the flour, salt, baking soda, cinnamon, allspice, ground ginger, and grated ginger. In another large bowl, using an electric mixer, beat together the butter and brown sugar until light and creamy. Beat in the egg. Add the molasses and beat until well blended, about 2 minutes. Beat in the flour mixture in three additions alternately with the buttermilk in two additions, beginning and ending with the flour mixture. Pour the batter into the prepared pan.

Bake until a toothpick inserted into the center of the cake comes out clean, about 50 minutes. Transfer to a wire rack and let cool in the pan for 10 minutes, then turn out of the pan, slipping a knife between edges of the cake and the pan to loosen any stuck edges. Turn the cake right side up and let cool for at least 15 minutes before serving.

Meanwhile, make the whipped cream, if using: In a large bowl, using an electric mixer, beat the cream until soft peaks form. Sprinkle in the confectioners' sugar and 1 tablespoon of the nutmeg and continue to beat until almost stiff peaks form. Cover and refrigerate until ready to serve the cake.

Serve the cake warm, cut into wedges. Top each wedge with a generous dollop of whipped cream and garnish with a sprinkle of the reserved nutmeg.

Wedges of this picture-perfect dessert, with their precisely patterned crust and rich chocolate interior, make a grand finale to a holiday meal. The crostata can also be cut into bite-sized pieces and served on your holiday buffet table.

Chocolate-Pecan Crostata

serves 10

2 ½ cups (10 oz/315 g) pecans

2 rolls store-bought pie pastry dough, each about 13 inches (33 cm) in diameter and ¼ inch (6 mm) thick, thawed in the refrigerator

2 tablespoons unsalted butter, melted

½ cup (3 ½ oz/105 g) firmly packed light brown sugar

2 large eggs

1 teaspoon vanilla extract (essence)

6 oz (185 g) semisweet (plain) chocolate, coarsely chopped

Confectioners' (icing) sugar for dusting

prep tip

For a lattice top with fluted edges, use a fluted pastry wheel to cut the strips of dough.

Preheat the oven to 350°F (180°C). Spread the pecans in a single layer on a baking sheet and bake, stirring once or twice, until fragrant and lightly toasted, 10–12 minutes. Pour onto a plate and let cool, then chop and set aside.

On a lightly floured work surface, roll out 1 dough disk into a round ⅛ inch (3 mm) thick, and then trim the round to 12 inches (30 cm) in diameter. Press it into a 9- or 10-inch (23- or 25-cm) fluted tart pan with a removable bottom and trim the edges evenly. Set aside.

In a bowl, combine the butter, brown sugar, eggs, and vanilla and stir until well blended. Stir in the pecans. Melt the chocolate in the top of a double boiler set over (but not touching) gently simmering water. Remove from the heat and let cool slightly, 2–3 minutes. Stir the chocolate into the egg mixture, blending well. Spoon the filling into the tart shell and smooth the surface with a spatula.

Roll out the second dough disk into a round about ⅛ inch (3 mm) thick, and then trim to 12 inches (30 cm) in diameter. Cut into strips about ⅜ inch (1 cm) wide. Lay the strips vertically across the crostata, spacing them 1–1 ½ inches (2.5–4 cm) apart. Repeat with more strips, laying them horizontally across the first strips on a slight diagonal to make a lattice. Trim the edges.

Bake until the crust is golden and the chocolate has puffed slightly and gone from glossy to dull, 17–20 minutes. Transfer to a wire rack and let cool. Using a fine-mesh sieve, sprinkle a light dusting of confectioners' (icing) sugar evenly over the top of the *crostata*. Remove the sides of the pan and cut into wedges. Serve warm or at room temperature.

An aromatic mix of ground spices such as mace, ginger, nutmeg, and cinnamon in the creamy filling and a gingersnap crust infuse this cheesecake with a heady bouquet of flavors. Allow time for chilling the cake overnight before serving.

Pumpkin-Ginger Cheesecake

serves 12

CRUST

2 ½ cups (6 oz/185 g) finely ground gingersnap cookies

¾ cup (5 oz/155 g) finely ground walnuts

¼ cup (2 oz/60 g) granulated sugar

5 tablespoons (2 ½ oz/75 g) unsalted butter, melted

FILLING

1 lb (500 g) cream cheese, at room temperature

¾ cup (6 oz/185 g) firmly packed light brown sugar

2 large eggs

3 ⅓ cups (26 ½ oz/830 g) pumpkin purée

½ cup (4 fl oz/125 ml) heavy (double) cream

1 teaspoon ground cinnamon

½ teaspoon *each* ground mace, ground ginger, and freshly grated nutmeg

Preheat the oven to 325°F (165°C) and wrap the outside of a 9-inch (23-cm) springform pan with aluminum foil. To make the crust, in a large bowl, combine the cookies, walnuts, granulated sugar, and butter and mix well. Pour the mixture into a springform pan. Using your fingertips, push all but a thin coating of the mixture toward the sides of the pan and then about 1 ½ inches (4 cm) up the sides. The edges will be slightly irregular. Bake until lightly browned, about 15 minutes. Transfer to a wire rack to cool slightly, and then refrigerate to cool completely before filling.

To make the filling, in a large bowl, using an electric mixer, beat together the cream cheese and brown sugar until well blended. Beat in the eggs, one at a time, until the mixture is smooth and uniform, about 3 minutes. Set aside ¼ cup (2 fl oz/60 ml). In another large bowl, stir together the pumpkin purée, cream, and spices until well blended, about 2 minutes. Add the larger portion of the cream cheese mixture to the pumpkin mixture and beat until well blended, about 2 minutes. Pour the filling into the crust. Pour the reserved cream cheese mixture into the center. With the tip of a butter knife, swirl the mixture gently in a circular motion to make a pattern on the surface.

Fill a baking pan with hot tap water to a depth of 1 inch (2.5 cm) and carefully place the foil-wrapped springform pan in it. Bake until only the center barely jiggles when the springform pan is shaken, about 50 minutes. Remove the cheesecake from the water bath and let cool to room temperature on a wire rack. Cover and refrigerate overnight.

To serve, run a knife around the edge of the pan, and then release the sides, leaving the bottom of the pan in place. Serve chilled, cut into wedges.

Dried cranberries add holiday color and a hint of tartness to a classic pear crisp. Make sure the pears are ripe, so that they will soften as they cook. Apples, especially Granny Smith or pippins, can be used in place of the pears.

Cranberry and Pear Crisp

serves 6–8

2 lb (1 kg) firm but ripe Barlett (Williams') or Bosc pears

2 teaspoons fresh lemon juice

½ cup (2 oz/60 g) dried cranberries

¾ cup (4 oz/125 g) all-purpose (plain) flour

⅔ cup (5 oz/155 g) firmly packed light brown sugar

⅛ teaspoon salt

4 tablespoons (2 oz/60 g) cold unsalted butter, diced

Whipped cream for serving (optional)

prep tip

The pears can be prepared up to 2 hours ahead of time and kept in cold water with 1 tablespoon lemon juice. Drain and pat dry before using.

Preheat the oven to 375°F (190°C). Lightly butter an 8-inch (20-cm) square or round baking dish.

Peel and core the pears and cut them lengthwise into slices ½ inch (12 mm) thick. Arrange them in the prepared baking dish and drizzle with the lemon juice, turning them once or twice. Scatter with the dried cranberries, tucking them among the pears.

In a bowl, stir together the flour, brown sugar, and salt. Add the butter and, using a pastry cutter or two knives, cut the butter into the flour mixture until the mixture is the size of small peas. Sprinkle the topping over the fruit.

Bake until the top is golden and the juices are bubbling around the edges, about 50 minutes. Transfer to a wire rack and let cool for 10–15 minutes.

Serve the crisp warm, scooping it directly from the baking dish. Accompany it with whipped cream, if desired.

The secret to this rich brownie cake is good-quality chocolate with a high cacao content. Decorate the cake by stenciling a pattern on top or by serving fresh berries alongside. See pages 222–223 for more decorating ideas.

Rich Chocolate Brownie Cake

serves 8–10

½ cup (4 oz/125 g) unsalted butter, at room temperature

1 cup (8 oz/250 g) sugar

2 large eggs, lightly beaten

1 teaspoon vanilla extract (essence)

⅛ teaspoon salt

¾ cup (4 oz/125 g) all-purpose (plain) flour

4 oz (125 g) good-quality semisweet (plain) or bittersweet chocolate, at least 61 percent cacao, coarsely chopped

Confectioners' (icing) sugar for dusting

shopping tip

When purchasing chocolate, the higher the percentage of cacao, the more bitter the chocolate will be. For a deeper-flavored cake, choose bittersweet chocolate with at least 71 percent cacao.

Photos on pages 222–223

Preheat the oven to 350°F (180°C). Line an 8-inch (20-cm) round cake pan with a piece of aluminum foil, allowing the edge to overlap the pan. Using a pastry brush, lightly butter the foil.

In a large bowl, using an electric mixer, beat the butter until light and fluffy, about 1 minute. Add the sugar and beat until well blended. Add the eggs and vanilla and beat again until well blended. Add the salt and ¼ cup (1 ½ oz/45 g) of the flour and beat well. Add the remaining flour in two batches, beating well after each addition.

Melt the chopped chocolate in the top of a double boiler set over (but not touching) gently simmering water. Remove from the heat and let cool slightly, 2–3 minutes. Add it to the cake batter and beat until well blended and creamy. Pour the batter into the prepared pan, smoothing the surface with a spatula.

Bake until the cake is puffed and a toothpick inserted into its center comes out clean, 20–25 minutes. Transfer to a wire rack and let cool completely.

Using the edges of the foil, lift the cooled cake out of the pan. Invert the cake onto a cake stand or cake plate and peel off the foil. Turn the cake right side up. Place a stencil of your choice on top, and then sift the confectioners' sugar over the stencil to create a pattern. Carefully lift off the stencil.

To serve, slice into wedges.

Ideas for Decorating Cakes

using a template

You can buy stencils in cookware stores, or make your own by drawing shapes on a piece of tracing or heavy-stock paper and then cutting them out. You can choose any shape you like, such as a spiral, star, dove, snowflake, tree, or leaf. To decorate your cake, place a stencil on top and, using a fine-mesh sieve, dust the stencil with confectioners' sugar or cocoa powder.

plate decorations

To create a snowy effect, decorate your serving plate or cake stand with berries that are dusted with confectioners' sugar. Any type of berries or small citrus fruits will work. Candied rose petals or violets can also be used.

cocoa powder

For a dramatic effect, place cocoa powder in a fine-mesh sieve and dust the top of the cake and the sides of the serving plate.

chocolate shavings

Use a vegetable peeler to make chocolate shavings and place them on top of the cake and around the edge of the cake plate. Use white or dark chocolate, or a mixture.

Apple Tarte Tatin

serves 8

TART PASTRY

2 cups (10 oz/315 g) all-purpose (plain) flour

1 teaspoon salt

½ cup (4 oz/125 g) plus 2 tablespoons cold unsalted butter, cut into ½-inch (12-mm) pieces

6 tablespoons (3 fl oz/90 ml) ice water

FILLING

4 ½–5 lb (2.25–2.5 kg) firm baking apples such as Northern Spy or Golden Delicious, peeled, halved, and cored

3 tablespoons fresh lemon juice

1 ½ cups (12 oz/375 g) sugar

½ cup (4 oz/125 g) plus 2 tablespoons unsalted butter, cut into thin slices

serving tip

Serve this dessert with Cinnamon-Spiced Whipped Cream (page 207) or vanilla ice cream.

To make the pastry, in a food processor, combine the flour and salt and pulse once or twice to blend. Add the butter pieces and pulse or process until the mixture is the size of small peas, about 45 seconds. Add the ice water and pulse several times, just until a loose ball has formed. Remove the dough, pat gently into a disk, wrap in plastic wrap, and refrigerate for 15 minutes.

On a lightly floured surface, roll the dough out into a round 12 inches (30 cm) in diameter. Lay the dough round on a sheet of plastic wrap and cover with a second sheet. Refrigerate while preparing the apples.

To make the filling, drizzle the apple halves with the lemon juice. Sprinkle the sugar in the bottom of a heavy, 10-inch (25-cm) cast-iron or other ovenproof frying pan. Lay the butter slices on top of the sugar. Starting from the outer edge, arrange the apple halves, cut side up and stem ends facing inward, in concentric circles, ending with a single half in the center. To fit as many apples as possible, tip them slightly on their edges.

Place the frying pan over medium-low heat and cook the apples in the butter until a golden brown sauce has formed and the apples are almost tender. As the butter melts and begins to form a sauce, baste the apples with it. They will gradually absorb the caramelized syrup. This process will take about 1 hour. If the apples are cooking too quickly, reduce the heat to low and continue to baste often. Preheat the oven to 425°F (220°C) after about 45 minutes.

When the apples are ready, remove the pastry from the refrigerator and unwrap it. Lay it over the apples, tucking it down and over them around the side of the pan. Place the assembled tart (still in the pan) on a baking sheet. Bake until the crust is golden, 20–25 minutes.

Transfer to a wire rack and let cool for 10 minutes. Slide a knife along the inside edge of the frying pan to loosen any bits of sticking apple or crust. Invert a flat serving platter on top of the frying pan. Wearing oven mitts and holding the platter and the frying pan firmly together, carefully and quickly invert them so the platter is on the bottom. Lift off the pan. If any apple clings to it, simply remove and place on the tart. Cut into wedges and serve warm.

No one can resist ice cream, especially when it is homemade. For this ice cream to be its best, store it in the freezer for at least 6 hours before serving, giving it time to develop its optimal texture and a more intense flavor.

Cinnamon Ice Cream

serves 6

2 cups (16 fl oz/500 ml) heavy (double) cream

2 cups (16 fl oz/500 ml) whole milk

1 ¼ cups (9 oz/280 g) firmly packed light brown sugar

¼ teaspoon salt

4 cinnamon sticks, plus 6–8 for garnish

4 large egg yolks

1 tablespoon ground cinnamon

serving tip

Make ice cream sandwiches by spreading a small scoop of ice cream between 2 Sugar Cookies (page 256) or Chewy Ginger-Molasses Cookies (page 260).

In a large, heavy-bottomed saucepan over medium-high heat, combine the cream, milk, brown sugar, salt, and 4 cinnamon sticks. Heat, stirring often, until the brown sugar has dissolved. In a small bowl, whisk the egg yolks until thickened and pale. Gradually whisk about 1 cup (8 fl oz/250 ml) of the hot milk mixture into the yolks. Whisk the hot yolk mixture into the hot cream mixture and cook, stirring constantly until the mixture is thick enough to coat the back of a spoon, 4–5 minutes. Remove from the heat and let cool to room temperature. Remove and discard the cinnamon sticks, and stir in the ground cinnamon.

Freeze the custard in an ice-cream maker according to the manufacturer's directions. You should have about 1 qt (1 l).

To serve, scoop into bowls and garnish with a cinnamon stick.

The deep magenta juice of the blood orange, with its slight raspberry flavor, makes a bright finish to a holiday meal. You can make the sugar syrup up two weeks in advance and refrigerate it in a tightly covered container.

Blood Orange Granita

serves 6–8

1 ½ cups (12 fl oz/375 ml) water

1 cup (8 oz/250 g) sugar

1 tablespoon grated blood orange zest

2 cups (16 fl oz/500 ml) fresh blood orange juice

Lemon Zest Shortbread (page 251), optional

prep tip

Other types of citrus zest, such as grapefruit or Meyer lemon, can be substituted for the blood orange zest.

In a small saucepan over medium-high heat, stir together the water, sugar, and orange zest. Bring to a boil and cook, stirring occasionally, until the sugar dissolves, about 5 minutes. Remove from the heat and let cool to room temperature. Cover and refrigerate until well chilled, about 3 hours.

In a large bowl, combine the chilled sugar syrup and blood orange juice and mix until well blended. Pour into a 9-by-13-inch (23-by-33-cm) nonaluminum metal baking pan. Put the pan in the freezer. After about 1 hour, when the mixture starts to get icy around the edges, use a fork to break up the ice crystals, working from the edges to the center of the pan. Return to the freezer. From that point, scrape the mixture with a fork every 30–40 minutes until it forms fine, firm, icy flakes, 2–3 hours longer.

Scoop the icy flakes into chilled bowls or glasses and serve at once, accompanied with the shortbread, if desired. Although granita tastes best when eaten the same day it is made, leftovers can be frozen for up to 3 days. To serve, let stand at room temperature for 5 minutes to soften slightly and then scrape again with a fork to lighten the texture.

Making these truffles, a fun dessert for kids, calls for only a handful of easy steps. The truffles can be made up to a week in advance, which leaves you plenty of time for preparing last-minute dishes on the day of your holiday dinner.

Ice Cream Truffles

makes 24 truffles

1 cup (5 ½ oz/170 g) almonds, pecans, macadamia nuts, pistachios, or walnuts

1 pt (16 fl oz/500 ml) vanilla ice cream

12 oz (375 g) good-quality semisweet (plain) chocolate, at least 61 percent cacao, coarsely chopped

serving tip

Ice cream in any flavor, such as chocolate or strawberry, can be used. Serve the truffles on footed dessert dishes or in small, decorative bowls.

Preheat the oven to 350°F (180°C). Place the nuts in a single layer on a baking sheet and bake, stirring once or twice, until lightly toasted, 10–12 minutes. Transfer to a plate and let cool and then chop coarsely and set aside.

Line a baking sheet with aluminum foil. Using a small ice-cream scoop or a tablespoon, scoop out balls of the ice cream (about 1 inch/2.5 cm in diameter) and place them on the prepared baking sheet. Work quickly, making 24 balls total. Cover the baking sheet with foil and freeze for up to 24 hours.

When you are ready to coat the ice-cream balls, melt the chocolate in the top of a double boiler set over (but not touching) gently simmering water. Remove from the heat and set aside.

Place a wire rack on a baking sheet or a sheet of aluminum foil, and then transfer the ice-cream balls to the rack. Spoon some of the chocolate over each ball, rolling the ball as needed to coat on all sides. Sprinkle the balls with nuts while the chocolate is still soft.

Return the coated balls to the foil-lined baking sheet, cover, and freeze until ready to serve. They can be frozen for up to 1 week.

To serve, place a few balls on a plate or in a bowl and serve at once.

Breakfast

232   Grapefruit Compote with Fresh Mint

233   Frittata with Spinach, Roasted Red Peppers, and Gruyère

235   Scrambled Eggs with Mushrooms, Cheddar, and Pancetta

236   Sausages with Sautéed Apples and Onions

237   Twice-Cooked Potatoes with Fresh Herbs

238   Soufflé Ricotta Pancakes with Orange Maple Syrup

240   Buttermilk-Blueberry Scone Bites

241   Cranberry Cornmeal Muffins

242   Cinnamon Coffee Bundt Cake

In France and Italy, wild mushrooms are commonly incorporated into omelets with various cheeses or cured meats and served for a light lunch or dinner. Here, that same combination is used for a hearty breakfast dish.

Scrambled Eggs with Mushrooms, Cheddar, and Pancetta

serves 6–8

4 tablespoons (2 oz/60 g) unsalted butter

½ lb (250 g) wild mushrooms such as chanterelle, porcini (ceps), or black trumpet, brushed clean and coarsely chopped

1 teaspoon sea salt

10 large eggs

½ teaspoon freshly ground pepper

1 clove garlic, minced

2 oz (60 g) thinly sliced pancetta, cut into ½-inch (12-mm) pieces

¼ lb (125 g) Cheddar cheese, cut into ½-inch (12-mm) cubes

2 tablespoons minced fresh flat-leaf (Italian) parsley

prep tip

Fresh herbs, such as thyme or basil, can be used in place of the parsley, while Gruyère or mozzarella cheese can be substituted for the Cheddar.

In a frying pan over medium-high heat, melt 1 ½ tablespoons of the butter. When it foams, add the mushrooms and sauté until they release their juices, 4–5 minutes. Sprinkle with ¼ teaspoon of the salt. Using a slotted spoon, transfer to a bowl and set aside.

Break the eggs into a separate bowl, add the pepper and the remaining ¾ teaspoon salt, and whisk until well blended.

In a clean frying pan over medium heat, melt the remaining 2 ½ tablespoons butter. When it foams, add the garlic and pancetta and sauté until translucent, 2–3 minutes. Pour in the eggs and reduce the heat to low. Cook, stirring often, until the eggs are nearly cooked to the desired consistency, about 5 minutes for a soft curd and 7–8 minutes for a firmer one. Add the mushrooms, cheese, and parsley during the last 2 minutes of cooking.

Spoon the eggs onto a platter or individual plates and serve at once.

Onions and apples add a sweet note to the savory sausage, and deglazing the pan with apple cider and balsamic vinegar before serving adds to the complexity of this simple breakfast dish.

Sausages with Sautéed Apples and Onions

serves 6–8

2 tablespoons unsalted butter

2 ½ lb (1.25 kg) sausages such as chicken-apple or mild Italian

2 tablespoons water

2 large yellow onions, cut into slices ¼ inch (6 mm) thick

4 or 5 large, firm apples such as Granny Smith or Gala, peeled, halved, cored, and cut lengthwise into slices ¼ inch (6 mm) thick

½ teaspoon sea salt

½ teaspoon freshly ground pepper

2 tablespoons apple cider

2 teaspoons balsamic vinegar

serving tip

Serve alongside breakfast foods such as eggs, pancakes, or waffles.

Preheat the oven to 200°F (95°C).

In a large frying pan over medium-high heat, melt 1 tablespoon of the butter. When it foams, add the sausage, reduce the heat to medium, and brown on 1 side, about 4 minutes. Turn and cook on the other side until browned, about 5 minutes longer. Reduce the heat to low, add the water, cover, and simmer until the juice runs clear when the sausage is pierced with a fork, about 5 minutes. Transfer the sausages to an ovenproof dish and place in the warm oven while you cook the apples and onions.

Pour off all but 1 tablespoon of the juices in the frying pan. Add the remaining 1 tablespoon butter and melt over medium-high heat. When it foams, add the onions and cook, stirring often, until translucent, 4–5 minutes. Add the apples and stir to coat with the butter. Continue stirring often until the onions and apples are tender and golden, about 8 minutes. Sprinkle with the salt and pepper, and then pour in the apple cider and scrape the pan bottom to loosen the browned bits. Stir in the balsamic vinegar.

Return the sausages to the pan with the apples and onions and turn them several times to coat them with the pan juices.

To serve, spoon the apples and onions onto warmed individual plates or a warmed platter and top with the sausages. Serve at once.

In this recipe, the potatoes are first boiled and cooled, and then sliced and given a second cooking in butter and olive oil, where they develop a golden crust. You can boil and cool the potatoes up to 24 hours in advance.

Twice-Cooked Potatoes with Fresh Herbs

serves 8

8–10 Yukon gold or white potatoes, about 1 ½ lb (750 g) total weight

2 tablespoons sea salt

2 tablespoons unsalted butter

3 tablespoons extra-virgin olive oil

1 tablespoon minced fresh flat-leaf (Italian) parsley

1 teaspoon minced fresh marjoram or oregano

2 teaspoons minced fresh chives

shopping tip

Other types of potatoes, such as Yellow Finn or small red potatoes, can be used in place of the Yukon golds.

Photo on page 230

Put the potatoes and 1 tablespoon of the salt in a large pot and add water to cover by 3 inches (7.5 cm). Bring to a boil over medium-high heat and cook just until tender when pierced with a knife, 25–30 minutes. Do not overcook. Remove and let cool slightly before removing the skins. Let cool completely, and then cut into slices ½ inch (12 mm) thick. Cover and refrigerate until you are ready to fry them.

Select a frying pan large enough to accommodate the potato slices in a single layer. (Alternatively, fry the potatoes in two batches or use two frying pans.) Place the pan over medium-high heat and add the butter and olive oil. When the butter starts to foam, arrange the sliced potatoes in the pan in a single layer, sprinkle them with 1 ½ teaspoons of the salt, and cook until golden on the bottom, 7–8 minutes. Turn, sprinkle with the remaining 1 ½ teaspoons salt, and cook until golden on the second side, about 5 minutes. Sprinkle with the herbs and turn the potatoes once or twice to coat them with the herbs.

Transfer the potatoes to paper towels to drain briefly. Transfer to a platter, garnish with the fresh chives and serve hot.

These pancakes are especially light because of the egg whites. The maple syrup is flavored with an infusion of fresh oranges, but you can substitute 2 tablespoons orange blossom water. The syrup can be made up to 3 days in advance.

Soufflé Ricotta Pancakes with Orange Maple Syrup

serves 4–6

ORANGE MAPLE SYRUP

1 orange, cut into eight wedges

1 cup (8 fl oz/250 ml) water

1 teaspoon honey

2 cups (22 oz/680 g)
pure maple syrup

1 ½ cups (7 ½ oz/235 g)
all-purpose (plain) flour

1 teaspoon baking soda
(bicarbonate of soda)

1 teaspoon baking powder

½ teaspoon salt

2 tablespoons sugar

3 large eggs, separated

1 ⅓ cups (11 fl oz/345 ml) buttermilk

½ cup (4 oz/125 g) ricotta, drained
in a sieve for 1 hour

Unsalted butter for frying

To make the orange maple syrup, in a saucepan over high heat, combine the orange wedges, water, and honey and bring to a boil. Reduce the heat to medium-low and simmer until the liquid is reduced to ½ cup (4 fl oz/125 ml). Strain into a clean saucepan, add the maple syrup, and stir over low heat to combine. Set aside.

Preheat the oven to 200°F (95°C). Place a platter in the oven to warm.

In a large bowl, whisk together the flour, baking soda, baking powder, and salt until blended. In a medium bowl, whisk together the sugar, egg yolks, buttermilk, and ricotta until smooth. In another medium bowl, using an electric mixer, beat the egg whites until soft peaks form.

Add the buttermilk mixture into the flour mixture and stir just until blended. Stir in 2–3 tablespoons of the egg whites to lighten the mixture, and then fold in the remaining egg whites, being careful not to deflate the batter too much.

Heat a griddle or nonstick frying pan over medium-high heat. When hot, add ½ teaspoon of butter. Using a ¼ cup (2 fl oz/60 ml) measure, pour the batter onto the griddle, spacing the pancakes about 2 inches (5 cm) apart. Cook until the pancakes are golden on the underside and small bubbles appear on the top, about 2 minutes. Turn over and cook the other side until golden, 1–2 minutes longer. Carefully transfer each pancake to the warmed platter. Repeat with the remaining batter, adding more butter as needed.

Serve warm with the orange maple syrup.

These bite-sized scones are a welcome accompaniment to any savory breakfast dish. Pass them at the table or place them on a sideboard with store-bought lemon curd. Raspberries can be substituted for the blueberries.

Buttermilk-Blueberry Scone Bites

makes 36 bite-sized scones

3 ½ cups (17 ½ oz/545 g) all-purpose (plain) flour

½ cup (4 oz/125 g) plus 1 tablespoon sugar

1 teaspoon baking powder

½ teaspoon baking soda (bicarbonate of soda)

1 tablespoon minced lemon zest

1 cup (8 oz/250 g) cold unsalted butter, cut into 1-inch (2.5-cm) pieces

½ cup (4 fl oz/125 ml) buttermilk

½ cup (4 oz/125 g) nonfat plain yogurt

2 ½ cups (10 oz/315 g) fresh or well-drained thawed, frozen blueberries

1 tablespoon whole milk

serving tip

These miniature scone bites are also a nice addition to a holiday brunch buffet or tea party.

Preheat the oven to 325°F (165°C). Have ready an ungreased baking sheet.

In a large bowl, whisk together the flour, ½ cup sugar, and the baking powder, baking soda, and lemon zest. Add the butter and, using a pastry blender, cut the butter into the flour mixture until the mixture is the size of peas.

In a small bowl, stir together the buttermilk and yogurt until well blended. Drizzle some of the buttermilk mixture over the flour mixture and toss with a fork just to incorporate the ingredients. Continue to add the buttermilk mixture slowly, tossing with a fork, until it has all been incorporated and the flour mixture is evenly moist. Scatter the blueberries on top and mix them in with your fingertips. Gather the dough into a ball.

On a lightly floured work surface, roll out the dough in a circle about 1 inch (2.5 cm) thick. Using a 2-inch (5-cm) biscuit cutter, cut into rounds. Cut each round into quarters to make bite-sized wedges. Arrange the wedges on the baking sheet. Brush the top of each wedge with the milk and then sprinkle with the 1 tablespoon sugar.

Bake until the scones are lightly browned, about 25 minutes. Serve warm.

Cranberries are a sign of the holiday season, and can be used in a myriad of ways, from sauce to dessert. Here, they provide tart-sweet bits of color for breakfast muffins that are best served warm from the oven.

Cranberry Cornmeal Muffins

makes 12 muffins

1 cup (5 oz/155 g) all-purpose (plain) flour

½ cup (2 ½ oz/75 g) cornmeal

⅔ cup (5 oz/155 g) sugar

1 tablespoon baking powder

½ teaspoon salt

2 large eggs

1 cup (8 fl oz/250 ml) whole milk

2 tablespoons corn oil

4 tablespoons (2 oz/60 g) unsalted butter, melted

1 tablespoon grated orange zest

1 tablespoon fresh orange juice

1 cup (4 oz/125 g) fresh cranberries, chopped

shopping tip

Other berries, such as raspberries, strawberries, or blackberries, can be used in place of the cranberries.

Preheat the oven to 400°F (200°C). Line a standard 12-cup muffin pan with paper liners or butter lightly.

In a large bowl, combine the flour, cornmeal, sugar, baking powder, and salt and whisk to mix well. In another bowl, combine the eggs, milk, corn oil, melted butter, orange zest, and orange juice and whisk to mix well. Gently mix in the cranberries. Pour the cranberry mixture into the flour mixture and stir just until the ingredients combine into a lumpy batter. Do not overmix. Spoon the batter into the prepared muffin cups, filling just to the rims.

Bake until a toothpick inserted into the center of a muffin comes out clean, 18–20 minutes. Transfer the pan to a wire rack and let cool for about 5 minutes.

Turn the muffins out of the pan and serve hot or warm.

Cinnamon Coffee Bundt Cake

serves 12–16

STREUSEL FILLING

¾ cup (3 oz/90 g) pecans or walnuts

2 tablespoons unsalted butter,
at room temperature

3 tablespoons all-purpose (plain) flour

⅓ cup (2 ½ oz/75 g) firmly packed
light brown sugar

1 ½ teaspoons ground cinnamon

BATTER

2 ½ cups (12 ½ oz/390 g) all-purpose
(plain) flour

2 teaspoons baking powder

½ teaspoon baking soda
(bicarbonate of soda)

½ teaspoon salt

¾ cup (6 oz/185 g) unsalted butter,
at room temperature

1 ¼ cups (10 oz/315 g) granulated sugar

4 large eggs

1 teaspoon vanilla extract (essence)

1 ½ cups (12 oz/375 g) sour cream

Confectioners' (icing) sugar for dusting

Preheat the oven to 350°F (180°C). Butter a 10-inch (25-cm) Bundt pan and then dust with flour and shake out the excess.

To make the streusel filling, place the nuts in a single layer on a baking sheet and bake, stirring once or twice, until lightly toasted, 10–12 minutes. Transfer to a plate and let cool, and then chop coarsely. Leave the oven on.

In a small bowl, combine the butter, flour, brown sugar, nuts, and cinnamon. Using a pastry blender or fork, mix until crumbly. Set the streusel aside.

To make the batter, in a large bowl, stir together the flour, baking powder, baking soda, and salt. Set aside.

To make by hand: In a large bowl, using a wooden spoon, beat together the butter and granulated sugar until light and creamy. Mix in the eggs and vanilla, beating until smooth and well blended. Add the flour mixture to the butter mixture in three batches alternately with the sour cream in two batches, beginning and ending with the flour mixture and stirring with a rubber spatula just until blended and almost smooth.

To make using an electric mixer: In a large bowl, beat together the butter and granulated sugar on medium-low speed until creamy. Beat in the eggs one at a time, mixing well after each addition. Stir in the vanilla. Add the flour mixture to the butter mixture in three batches alternately with the sour cream in two batches, beginning and ending with the flour mixture and beating on low speed just until blended and almost smooth.

Pour half of the batter into the prepared pan and smooth the surface with a rubber spatula. Sprinkle evenly with half the streusel filling. Cover with the remaining batter and sprinkle with the remaining streusel.

Bake until a toothpick inserted into the center of the cake comes out clean, 40–45 minutes. Let cool in the pan on a wire rack for 10 minutes, and then turn out of the pan and let cool completely. The cake will keep in an airtight container at room temperature for up to 3 days. To serve, using a fine-mesh sieve, dust with confectioners' sugar; cut the cake into wedges.

Gifts from the Kitchen

Ideas for Packaging Gifts **247**

Chocolate-Marshmallow Fudge **248**

Pistachio Brittle **250**

Lemon Zest Shortbread **251**

Coconut Macaroons **253**

Ideas for Decorating Cookies **254**

Sugar Cookies **256**

Royal Icing **257**

Chocolate Ganache Filling **257**

Caramel Sea Salt Truffles **258**

260 Chewy Ginger-Molasses Cookies

261 Fig and Walnut Quick Bread

263 Chocolate Cranberry-Pistachio Biscotti

264 Chocolate-Peppermint Crinkles

266 Candied Grapefruit Peel

267 Blueberry Syrup

268 Spiced Rosemary Nuts

270 Blood Orange Marmalade

271 Preserved Lemons

273 Marinated Goat Cheese

Ideas for Packaging Gifts

votive holders

Fill a votive holder or shot glass with an edible gift. Choose clear glass or an assortment of sizes and colors. Tie a decorative ribbon and a small ornament around the bottom.

glass jars

Glass jars are the perfect vessels for cookies or confections. Cut out rounds of waxed paper and alternate the treats with the paper rounds. Fasten the jar lid on tightly, tie with a decorative bow, and attach a gift tag.

gift boxes

Put sweet treats in brightly colored boxes, or choose a patterned box. Wrap the food in festive paper and attach a gift tag. Alternatively, use metal tins or canisters.

This creamy, rich fudge is lightened by the marshmallows. The fudge will keep, uncut, in the refrigerator for 1 week, tightly wrapped in aluminum foil. Cut into bars or squares before serving or packing into gift boxes.

Chocolate-Marshmallow Fudge

makes sixteen 2-inch (2.5-cm) bars

4 tablespoons (2 oz/60 g) unsalted butter, melted

1 cup (7 oz/220 g) firmly packed light brown sugar

1 cup (8 oz/250 g) granulated sugar

¼ cup (2 ½ oz/75 g) light corn syrup

½ cup (4 fl oz/125 ml) half-and-half (half cream)

⅛ teaspoon salt

4 oz (125 g) bittersweet or semisweet (plain) chocolate, coarsely chopped

½ cup (2 oz/60 g) chopped walnuts

1 ½ cups (2 ½ oz/75 g) miniature marshmallows

Lightly butter an 8-inch (20-cm) square pan and set aside.

In a large, heavy saucepan over medium heat, combine the butter, sugars, corn syrup, half-and-half, and salt and bring to a boil, stirring constantly. Using a pastry brush dipped in hot water, brush down any sugar crystals that form on the sides of the pan. Boil for 2 ½ minutes and then stir in the chocolate until melted and well blended. Continue to boil, without stirring, until a candy thermometer reads 234°F (112°C), 7–10 minutes.

Remove from the heat and let cool until almost room temperature, or 110°F (43°C) on a candy thermometer, about 15 minutes. Using an electric mixer, beat the fudge until the color dulls and the fudge is creamy, 2–3 minutes. Mix in the walnuts by hand.

Sprinkle the marshmallows in the prepared pan and spoon the fudge over them. Lay a piece of plastic wrap across the surface and, using your hands, press the fudge down into the marshmallows. Remove the plastic and smooth the surface of the fudge with a spatula. Cover the pan with aluminum foil and refrigerate until firm, about 6 hours. Cut into 2-inch (2.5-cm) bars, or any shape desired, to serve or give as a gift.

These macaroons are perfect for gift giving, as they will stay fresh for up to 5 days. To achieve their chewy interior and firm exterior, they are left in the oven with the door ajar for several minutes after they have finished baking.

Coconut Macaroons

makes about 24 cookies

2 large egg whites

3 tablespoons sugar

1 teaspoon vanilla extract (essence)

3 cups (12 oz/375 g) sweetened shredded dried coconut, plus more for serving

½–¾ cup (4–6 fl oz/125–180 ml) sweetened condensed milk

Candied rose petals or violets (optional)

serving tip

Dress up these cookies by dipping half of each cookie in melted chocolate. Let the chocolate harden before serving.

Preheat the oven to 250°F (120°C). Line 2 rimmed baking sheets with parchment (baking) paper.

In a bowl, using an electric mixer, beat the egg whites until they just barely hold soft peaks. Beat in the sugar and vanilla and then continue beating until stiff peaks form. Set aside.

In a large bowl, mix together the coconut and just enough of the condensed milk to make a sticky batter. Fold in the egg white mixture.

Drop the batter by teaspoonfuls onto the prepared baking sheets, spacing them about 1 inch (2.5 cm) apart. Dip the spoon into cold water every once in a while to prevent the batter from sticking.

Bake until the cookies are golden, 25–30 minutes. Turn the oven off. Prop the oven door ajar and leave the cookies in the oven for another 10 minutes. Transfer the baking sheets to wire racks and let the cookies cool completely on the pans before removing.

If desired, serve on a bed of shredded coconut with a few candied rose petals or violets or both. Store in layers, separated by waxed paper, in an airtight container at room temperature for up to 5 days.

Ideas for Decorating Cookies

sprinkles

Use single-color sprinkles or a mixture of colors to add sparkle to sugar cookies. Colored sugars are sold in different-sized grains, from fine to coarse. The coarser ones are easier to work with. Apply to iced cookies by hand or with a spoon.

flooding

Flooding creates an even layer of frosting that won't run off the edge of the cookie. Use a pastry (piping) bag that is fitted with a narrow tip or a plastic bag with a hole cut in the corner. Fill the bag with Royal Icing (page 257) and outline the edge of the cookie to create a border (the icing must be fluid; add a little water if needed). Pipe icing into the middle of the cookie, letting it run to the edges of the border. Let the icing set.

create a design

Make a design by first flooding a cookie with icing. Before the icing has dried, add a dot of a different-colored icing in the center of the cookie. Use a toothpick to drag a design, such as a zigzag or spiral, on top.

make cookie sandwiches

Create sandwiches by spreading Chocolate Ganache Filling (page 257) between 2 cookies and then dusting with cocoa powder.

Sugar cookies are a holiday tradition in many households. They are delicious eaten plain and are even better when decorated with icing and sprinkles. Box up these cookies for friends and family for their holiday celebrations.

Sugar Cookies

Photos on pages 254–255

makes about 36 cookies

2/3 cup (5 oz/155 g) unsalted butter, at room temperature

1/2 cup (4 oz/125 g) granulated sugar

1 large egg

1 3/4 cups (9 oz/280 g) all-purpose (plain) flour

1/2 teaspoon baking powder

1/4 teaspoon salt

Royal Icing for decorating (page 257), optional

Chocolate Ganache Filling for cookie sandwiches (page 257), optional

prep tip

For extra flavor, add 2 teaspoons grated lemon or orange zest to the dough.

Photos on pages 254–255

Preheat the oven to 400°F (200°C). Have ready 2 ungreased baking sheets.

In a food processor, combine the butter and granulated sugar and pulse until creamy. Add the egg and pulse 5 or 6 times until fluffy and blended. In a small bowl, whisk together the flour, baking powder, and salt. Add one-third of the flour mixture to the food processor and process until blended, about 45 seconds. Add the remaining flour in two batches, processing after each addition until the dough is smooth.

Turn the dough out onto a well-floured work surface, shape into a ball, and then roll out 1/8 inch (3 mm) thick. Using cookie cutters, cut the dough into desired shapes. Then, using a spatula, transfer the cutouts to the baking sheets. Gather up the dough scraps, form into a ball, roll out and cut more shapes, and add to the baking sheets.

Bake until lightly browned on the bottom and pale golden on top, 6–8 minutes. Transfer to wire racks and let cool on the baking sheets for 5 minutes, and then transfer to the racks to cool completely.

Decorate the cooled cookies with Royal Icing, or use Chocolate Ganache Filling to make cookie sandwiches.

This snowy white icing is traditionally used for decorating holiday sugar cookies, and the ganache makes a delicious filling for your favorite cookie sandwiches. See pages 254–255 for ideas on how to decorate and fill cookies using these recipes.

Royal Icing

makes 1 cup
(8 fl oz/250 ml)

2 large egg whites

1 lb (500 g) confectioners' (icing) sugar, or more if needed

1 teaspoon water, if needed

Food coloring, optional

In a large bowl, using an electric mixer, beat together the egg whites and 1 lb confectioners' sugar until stiff enough to spread, about 10 minutes. If the icing is too stiff, beat in 1 teaspoon water. If it is too thin, continue beating for 2–3 minutes longer, or beat in another ¼ cup (1 oz/30 g) confectioners' sugar. Use immediately before the icing starts to thicken.

To make different-colored icings, divide the icing among several bowls and add food coloring as desired. (Start with just a drop of food coloring and go from there.) Using a knife or spatula, spread the icing on cookies.

Chocolate Ganache Filling

makes about 1⅓ cups
(11 fl oz/340 ml)

6 oz (185 g) bittersweet or semisweet (plain) chocolate, finely chopped

2 tablespoons unsalted butter

½ cup (4 fl oz/125 ml) heavy (double) cream

In a heatproof bowl, combine the chocolate and butter.

In a small saucepan over medium-high heat, bring the cream just to a boil. Remove from the heat and immediately pour over the chocolate and butter. Stir with a wire whisk until the chocolate and butter melt and are smooth. Let cool until spreadable.

Use immediately, or refrigerate for up to 2 days, and then bring to room temperature and whisk briefly before using.

Using coarse sea salt crystals on the caramel gives added texture and a burst of flavor to these candies, but fine sea salt can be used as well. You can also add a tiny sprinkle of sea salt to the chocolate coat for a sparkling finish.

Caramel Sea Salt Truffles

makes about 50 truffles

1 cup (8 oz/250 g) sugar

1 cup (10 oz/315 g) light corn syrup

½ cup (4 oz/125 g) unsalted butter

1 cup (8 fl oz/250 ml) heavy (double) cream

1–1 ½ tablespoons sea salt, plus more for sprinkling

12 oz (375 g) bittersweet or semisweet (plain) chocolate, coarsely chopped

Lightly butter an 8-inch (20-cm) square baking pan.

In a heavy saucepan over medium-low heat, combine the sugar, corn syrup, butter, and ½ cup (4 fl oz/125 ml) of the cream. Bring to a simmer, stirring constantly, and then cook, stirring, until a candy thermometer reads 240°F (115°C), about 7 minutes. Remove from the heat and drizzle in the remaining ½ cup cream, stirring to mix well. The mixture will bubble up slightly.

Return the pan to the heat and continue to cook until the thermometer reads 244°F (118°C), about 10 minutes longer. Remove from the heat and pour the mixture into the prepared pan.

Let stand for 1 ½–2 hours. The mixture should be firm to the touch, but not hard. Using a tablespoon, scoop out and form balls of caramel and place them on a sheet of aluminum foil. The caramel scraps can be gathered and shaped into balls by hand. Sprinkle each ball with a few grains of sea salt. Let stand for 1 hour before dipping.

Melt the chocolate in the top of a double boiler set over (but not touching) gently simmering water. Remove from the heat and set aside. Line 2 baking sheets with waxed paper and top each with a wire rack. Using a fork, dip the caramel balls one at a time into the chocolate, turning to coat. Transfer to the wire racks to cool. Add a sprinkle of salt to the top of each truffle and let stand until the chocolate is firm and set.

Store in layers, separated by waxed paper, in an airtight container at room temperature for up to 1 week.

These firm, yet chewy cookies will keep well for up to 2 weeks, making them both a practical and delicious gift from your kitchen. For an even richer color and more intense flavor, use dark molasses.

Chewy Ginger-Molasses Cookies

makes about 48 cookies

2 ½ cups (12 ½ oz/390 g) all-purpose (plain) flour

2 teaspoons baking soda (bicarbonate of soda)

1 teaspoon ground cinnamon

1 teaspoon ground cloves

¼ teaspoon salt

1 tablespoon peeled and grated fresh ginger

¾ cup (6 oz/80 g) unsalted butter, at room temperature

1 cup (7 oz/220 g) firmly packed dark brown sugar

1 large egg

¼ cup (2 ¾ oz/80 g) light molasses

½ cup (4 oz/125 g) granulated sugar

shopping tip

Dark molasses, which is less sweet, can be used in place of the light.

Preheat the oven to 375°F (190°C). Lightly butter 2 baking sheets.

In a large bowl, combine the flour, baking soda, cinnamon, cloves, salt, and ginger and whisk to mix well. Set aside.

In another large bowl, using an electric mixer, beat together the butter and brown sugar until fluffy. Beat in the egg and molasses until well blended. Stir in the flour mixture a little at a time until well blended.

Put the granulated sugar in a small, shallow bowl. Shape the dough into walnut-sized balls, and dip the top of each ball in the granulated sugar.

Arrange the balls, sugar side up, on the prepared baking sheets, spacing them about 1 inch (2.5 cm) apart. Bake until firm to the touch, 10–12 minutes. Transfer to wire racks and let cool.

Store in layers, separated by waxed paper, in an airtight container at room temperature for up to 2 weeks.

Chewy and sweet, figs add extra moisture and texture to this bread. Toast the bread and serve with butter or with a thick cherry jam. It also makes a good accompaniment to a cheese course.

Fig and Walnut Quick Bread

serves 10–12

2 cups (10 oz/315 g) all-purpose (plain) flour

2 teaspoons baking powder

¼ teaspoon salt

6 tablespoons (3 oz/90 g) unsalted butter, at room temperature

⅔ cup (5 oz/155 g) firmly packed dark brown sugar

2 large eggs

2 teaspoons grated lemon zest

2 cups (16 fl oz/500 ml) whole milk

½ lb (250 g) dried figs, coarsely chopped (about 1 cup/6 oz/185 g)

⅔ cup (2 ½ oz/ 75 g) chopped walnuts

shopping tip

Use coarsely chopped pitted dates in place of the figs, or use a mixture of figs and dates.

Preheat the oven to 350°F (180°C). Using a pastry brush, lightly butter an 8 ½-by-4 ½-inch (21.5-by-11.5-cm) loaf pan.

In a large bowl, combine the flour, baking powder, and salt and whisk to mix well. Set aside.

In another large bowl, using an electric mixer, beat together the butter and brown sugar until fluffy. Beat in the eggs until well blended. Stir in the lemon zest. Add the flour mixture to the butter mixture in three batches alternately with the milk in two batches, beginning and ending with the flour mixture and stirring until well blended. Stir in the figs and walnuts. Spoon the batter into the prepared loaf pan, and smooth the top with a rubber spatula.

Bake until the bread is golden and puffed and a toothpick inserted into the center comes out clean, about 50 minutes. Transfer to a rack and let cool in the pan for 15 minutes. Run a knife along the inside edges of the pan to loosen any sticking bits, and then turn the pan upside down into your hand and quickly set the loaf right side up on the rack to cool completely.

To store, wrap in plastic wrap and keep in a cool, dark place for up to 4 days.

Chocolate Cranberry-Pistachio Biscotti

makes about 30 biscotti

½ cup (2 oz/60 g) dried cranberries

3 cups (15 oz/470 g) all-purpose (plain) flour

2 teaspoons baking powder

½ teaspoon salt

4 tablespoons (2 oz/60 g) unsalted butter, at room temperature

1 cup (8 oz/250 g) plus 1 tablespoon sugar

2 teaspoons vanilla extract (essence)

4 large eggs

½ cup (2 oz/60 g) whole pistachios, plus finely chopped pistachios for dipping (optional)

1 teaspoon water

10 oz (315 g) bittersweet or semisweet (plain) chocolate, coarsely chopped

shopping tip

Dried cherries can be substituted for the cranberries.

Preheat the oven to 325°F (165°C). Have ready an ungreased baking sheet.

Put the cranberries in a small bowl and cover with warm water. Soak until plumped, about 15 minutes. Drain, pat dry, and set aside.

In a large bowl, combine the flour, baking powder, and salt and whisk to mix well. In another large bowl, using an electric mixer, beat together the butter, the 1 cup sugar, and the vanilla until fluffy and well blended, about 2 minutes. Beat in 3 of the eggs until well blended, about 2 minutes longer. Gradually stir in the flour mixture and beat until smooth, about 3 minutes. Stir in the cranberries and the whole pistachios.

On a lightly floured work surface, divide the dough in half. Shape each half into a log 11 inches (28 cm) long by 1 ½ inches (4 cm) in diameter. In a small bowl, beat together the remaining egg and the water. Brush the top of each log with the egg mixture, and then sprinkle with the 1 tablespoon sugar. Place the logs, well-spaced, on the baking sheet and press down to flatten slightly.

Bake until slightly colored and somewhat firm to the touch, about 25 minutes. Transfer the baking sheet to a wire rack. Leave the oven on.

When the logs are cool, after about 10 minutes, transfer them to a cutting board and cut on the diagonal into slices about ¾ inch (2 cm) thick. Put the slices, cut side down, on the baking sheet and return to the oven. Bake until lightly golden, about 6 minutes. Turn the slices over and bake until the second sides are golden, 5–6 minutes longer. Transfer to a wire rack and let cool.

Melt the chocolate in the top of a double boiler set over (but not touching) gently simmering water. Remove from the heat. Put the finely chopped pistachios in a small bowl. Working quickly, dip one-third of each cookie into the chocolate, and then dip the chocolate-covered tip into the pistachios. Return the cookie to the rack until the chocolate sets. Set the chocolate back over the double boiler to remelt the chocolate as necessary.

Store in layers, separated by waxed paper, in an airtight container at room temperature for up to 1 week.

Crinkles, with their snowy white confectioners' sugar coating and surprise dark chocolate interiors, are given an extra treatment for the holidays with a colorful topping of crushed peppermint candies.

Chocolate-Peppermint Crinkles

makes about 48 cookies

4 oz (125 g) unsweetened chocolate, coarsely chopped

2 cups (10 oz/315 g) all-purpose (plain) flour

2 teaspoons baking powder

¼ teaspoon salt

3 large eggs

1 ½ cups (12 oz/375 g) granulated sugar

½ cup (4 fl oz/125 ml) canola, sunflower, or other light vegetable oil

2 teaspoons vanilla extract (essence)

20–24 red-and-white peppermint candies

1 cup (4 oz/125 g) confectioners' (icing) sugar

Melt the chocolate in the top of a double boiler set over (but not touching) gently simmering water. Remove from the heat and let cool slightly.

In a large bowl, whisk together the flour, baking powder, and salt. In a large bowl, using an electric mixer, beat together the eggs and the granulated sugar until well blended. Add the oil, vanilla extract, and melted chocolate and beat again until well blended. Stir in the flour mixture just until fully incorporated. Cover and refrigerate until the dough is firm enough to shape, at least 2 hours and up to 24 hours.

Preheat the oven to 350°F (180°C). Have ready an ungreased baking sheet.

Place the peppermint candies between two sheets of aluminum foil and strike with a hammer or meat mallet, breaking them into large pieces. Then roll the candies with a rolling pin to crush them into small pieces. Set aside.

Put the confectioners' sugar in a shallow bowl. Pinch off a piece of dough and roll it into a ball about 1 inch (2.5 cm) in diameter. Roll the ball in the confectioners' sugar, coating evenly, and place it on the baking sheet. Repeat until all the dough is used, spacing the balls 1 inch (2.5 cm) apart.

Bake until the cookies have puffed up and the surface cracks, showing the chocolate beneath, 8–10 minutes. Let cool slightly on the pan, and then gently press some of the crushed peppermint all over each cookie. Transfer the cookies to wire racks and let cool completely. Store in layers, separated by waxed paper, in an airtight container at room temperature for up to 3 days.

This old-fashioned sweet was often a holiday kitchen gift from one family to another. For a fancy touch, dip about two-thirds of each peel into melted bittersweet chocolate and place on wire racks until the chocolate sets.

Candied Grapefruit Peel

makes about 36 pieces

2 large grapefruits, ruby red or other variety

2 cups (16 fl oz/500 ml) water

1 ½ cups (12 oz/375 g) sugar

shopping tip

Oranges can be used in place of the grapefruits.

Photo on page 246

Using a sharp knife, cut a thin slice from the top and bottom of each grapefruit to reveal the flesh. From the top to the bottom, score through the outer peel and thick white pith to the flesh, spacing the cuts about 1 inch (2.5 cm) apart. Peel the grapefruits. Cut each peel section lengthwise into long strips about ¼ inch (6 mm) wide. (Reserve the flesh for another use.)

In a large saucepan, combine the peels with water to cover by 2 inches (5 cm). Bring to a boil over high heat, then reduce the heat to medium. Simmer, uncovered, until only about 1 inch (2.5 cm) of water remains, about 1 hour. The peels will begin to soften and become translucent. Drain.

When the peels are almost ready, in another saucepan, combine the 2 cups water and 1 cup (8 oz/250 g) of the sugar. Bring to a boil over high heat and stir to dissolve the sugar, 3–4 minutes. Remove from the heat and stir the drained, still-warm peels into the syrup. Let stand for 6–8 hours at room temperature.

Return the pan to low heat, bring to a simmer, and cook until the peels have absorbed most of the syrup, about 30 minutes. During the last stages of cooking, watch carefully to prevent scorching or burning.

Using a slotted spoon, transfer the peels to a sheet of waxed paper, spreading them in a single layer. Let stand for about 12 hours to dry slightly.

Place the remaining ½ cup (4 oz/125 g) sugar in a small, shallow bowl. Roll the peels, one at a time, in the sugar to coat. Arrange in a single layer on a fresh piece of waxed paper and let dry for a few hours longer.

Store in layers, separated by waxed paper, in an airtight container at room temperature for up to 2 months.

Blueberry Syrup

makes about 5 cups
(40 fl oz/1.25 l)

7 cups (28 oz/875 g) fresh or
frozen blueberries, washed

2 tablespoons fresh lemon juice

5 cups (2 ½ lb/1.25 kg) sugar

prep tip

Other types of berries, such as
raspberries or blackberries, fresh
or frozen, can be substituted for
the blueberries in this recipe.

Put the blueberries in a large bowl. Using a whisk, crush them into a coarse purée. Alternatively, put them in a food processor and pulse 4 or 5 times. Put the crushed berries in a large, nonaluminum pan over medium-high heat. Stir in the lemon juice and bring the mixture to a boil, stirring occasionally. Boil for about 1 minute. Let cool for 10 minutes, then strain through a fine-mesh sieve. You should have about 5 cups (40 fl oz/1.25 l) juice. Discard the berry pulp and strain again, this time lining the sieve with cheesecloth (muslin).

Have ready hot, sterilized pint jars and their lids and rings (see note). Put the blueberry juice in a clean, nonaluminum pan and add the sugar. Bring to a boil over medium-high heat, stirring constantly. Boil for 1 minute, skimming off any foam that forms. Remove from the heat.

Ladle the syrup into hot, sterilized jars, filling to within 1 inch (2.5 cm) of the rim. Wipe the rim clean, top with a hot lid, and seal tightly with a screw band. Repeat with the remaining syrup. Place the jars, not touching, on a metal rack in a large pot, and add boiling water to cover by at least 1 inch (2.5 cm). Cover, return to a boil, and boil for 15 minutes.

Using tongs, carefully remove the jars from the hot water bath and let stand at room temperature until cool. To test the seal, press down on the center of a lid and then lift your finger. If the lid remains depressed, the seal is good. Store the sealed jars in a cool, dark place for up to 6 months. If the seal has failed, store in the refrigerator for up to 1 week.

Note: To sterilize jars, wash the jars and their lids in hot, soapy water and rinse well. Place the jars upright in a large pot. Fill the pot with hot water, covering the jars by 1 inch (2.5 cm). Cover the pot, bring to a boil, and boil for 10 minutes at altitudes of 1,000 feet (300 m) or less; add an additional minute of boiling time for each 1,000 feet of elevation gain. Remove from the heat and leave the jars in the hot water until ready to use. Place the lids in a small saucepan. Add water to cover, bring to a boil, and remove from the heat. Leave the lids in the hot water until ready to use.

The combination of rosemary, cumin, and cayenne pepper lends an irresistible flavor to toasted nuts. Pack these savory gifts in small decorative tins or in cellophane bags tied with a ribbon.

Spiced Rosemary Nuts

makes about 2½ cups
(10 oz/315 g)

2 ½ cups (10 oz/315 g) mixed raw nuts
such as pecans, walnuts, and peanuts

2 tablespoons olive oil

1 ½ tablespoons chopped
fresh rosemary

1 tablespoon sugar

1 ½ teaspoons ground cumin

1 teaspoon salt

1 teaspoon freshly ground black pepper

¼ teaspoon cayenne pepper

Preheat the oven to 300°F (150°C).

Place the nuts in a bowl. In a small, heavy saucepan over medium-low heat, warm the olive oil. Add the rosemary and stir until aromatic, about 1 minute. Pour the seasoned oil over the nuts. Add the sugar, cumin, salt, black pepper, and cayenne and stir to coat the nuts evenly. Transfer the nuts to a baking pan.

Bake, stirring occasionally, until the nuts are toasted, about 20 minutes. Transfer to a plate and let cool completely.

Store in an airtight container at room temperature for up to 4 days.

Nearly everyone likes a thick, chunky, pleasantly tart marmalade for spreading on their morning toast or warm-from-the-oven muffins. Here, brilliantly hued blood oranges yield a jewel-toned marmalade for the holidays.

Blood Orange Marmalade

makes 4 pt (2 l)

7 large blood oranges, quartered

2 lemons, quartered

11 cups (88 fl oz/2.75 l) water

7–8 cups (3 ½–4 lb/1.75–2 kg) sugar

shopping tip

This marmalade can also be made with navel oranges or, if you can find them, Seville oranges.

Place the fruit in a nonaluminum pot, add the water, and soak overnight. Remove the fruit and cut into slices about ⅛ inch (3 mm) thick. Return the fruit to the water, place the pot over high heat, and bring to a boil. Reduce the heat to medium-high and simmer uncovered, stirring occasionally, for 1 hour. Add the sugar, stirring until dissolved, and then continue to boil until the mixture reads 220°F (104°C) on a candy thermometer, 20–40 minutes longer. After about 20 minutes, the color will deepen to amber, and, as the temperature rises, the bubbles will become smaller.

Have ready hot, sterilized jars and their lids and rings (see note on page 267). Ladle the marmalade into a hot, sterilized jar, filling to within 1 inch (2.5 cm) of the rim. Wipe the rim clean, top with a hot lid, and seal tightly with a screw band. Repeat with the remaining marmalade. Place the jars, not touching, on a metal rack in a large pot, and add boiling water to cover by at least 1 inch (2.5 cm). Cover, return to a boil, and boil for 15 minutes.

Using tongs, carefully remove the jars from the hot water bath and let stand at room temperature until cool. To test the seal, press down on the center of a lid and then lift your finger. If the lid remains depressed, the seal is good. Store the sealed jars in a cool, dark place for up to 6 months. If the seal has failed, store in the refrigerator for up to 2 weeks.

Preserved spiced lemons are staples in the pantries of the Middle East and North Africa, where they find their way into stews, salads, and other dishes. Once opened, they will keep in the refrigerator for up to 3 months.

Preserved Lemons

makes 2 qt (2 l)

4 ½ qt (4 ½ l) water

7–10 slightly underripe lemons

⅔ cup (5 oz/155 g) sea salt

2 cinnamon sticks

4 teaspoons coriander seeds

2 teaspoons peppercorns

8 whole cloves

1 dried chile such as New Mexico or Long Red

About 1 cup (8 fl oz/250 ml) extra-virgin olive oil

shopping tip

Meyer lemons, which are sweeter, can also be used in this recipe.

Pour 3 qt (3 l) of the water into a nonaluminum saucepan and place over high heat. Bring to a boil and add the lemons. When the water returns to a boil, cook the lemons for 3–4 minutes. Drain and immerse the lemons in cold water until they are cool enough to handle. Drain again and set aside.

Have ready 2 hot, sterilized quart jars and their lids and rings (see note on page 267). In a nonaluminum saucepan, combine the remaining 1 ½ qt (1 ½ l) water and the salt, cinnamon, coriander, peppercorns, cloves, and chile. Bring to a boil over high heat, then remove from the heat.

Tightly pack the whole lemons into the sterilized jars. If you wish, you can halve or quarter the lemons lengthwise for a tighter fit. Ladle in the hot brine, including the spices, to within 1 ½ inches (4 cm) of the jar rims. Add the olive oil to within ½ inch (12 mm) of the rims. Wipe the rims clean, top with hot lids, and seal tightly with screw bands. Let stand at room temperature until cool. To test the seal, press down on the center of a lid and then lift your finger. If the lid remains depressed, the seal is good. Store sealed jars in a cool, dark place for at least 2 months before using, to allow the lemons to take on the flavors of the brine. They will keep for up to 6 months. If the seal has failed, store in the refrigerator for up to 3 months.

This savory gift from the kitchen is a welcome departure from holiday confections. Pack the goat cheese in glass jars and tie with a decorative ribbon. Attach a card on top with suggestions for serving.

Marinated Goat Cheese

makes 1 pint

About 10 oz (315 g) firm fresh goat cheese, whole, sliced, or formed into small balls

2 bay leaves

12 black peppercorns

1 teaspoon dried thyme

1 teaspoon dried rosemary

2 cups (16 fl oz/500 ml) extra-virgin olive oil

Put the cheese in a dry, sterilized (see note on page 267), lidded jar large enough for the cheese to be covered by the oil. Tuck in the bay leaves and sprinkle with the peppercorns, thyme, and rosemary.

Pour olive oil over the cheese and close the lid.

Store the cheese in a cool, dark place for up to 2 months. Once opened, store in the refrigerator for up to 1 month. Bring to room temperature before serving.

The Holiday Table

Whether you are hosting an elegant sit-down dinner or a casual buffet, the table is the heart of a holiday party. All you need to make it special are a few basic elements, a unified look, and a decorative accent or two. Here is a guide to the basics of setting a welcoming holiday table.

linens

A high-quality light-colored cotton or linen tablecloth with an 18-inch (45-cm) overhang suits any holiday gathering. For formal meals, use matching cloth napkins; for more casual occasions, white, colored, or printed cloth napkins are good choices. Fold the napkins in a simple, creative way, or embellish them with ribbons and a spray of seasonal flowers or greenery. For a layered look, use place mats directly on the table surface or on top of a tablecloth. A long table runner can add color, either on the table or over a tablecloth.

glassware

Use glasses of similar quality and style. Simple, clear glasses will work with any setting, but the holidays are a good time to introduce some colored pieces, such as amber or red tumblers. If you own crystal, its sparkle will enliven any holiday table.

water glasses Any glass that holds about 6 ounces (180 ml) can work as a water glass, including tumblers.

wineglasses Look for thin-walled glasses that make a ping when tapped. For more formal entertaining, set out a glass for each wine you will serve. Use traditional large tulip-shaped red-wine glasses, and smaller white-wine and dessert-wine glasses, or simply go with a standard 10-ounce (310-ml) white-wine glass—a versatile choice that can be used for any kind of wine. Stemless wineglasses are now an attractive option.

party glassware Champagne flutes look festive, and their tall shape helps trap air bubbles, enhancing the wine's effervescence. Stemmed glasses with V-shaped bowls are used for any mixed drink served without ice. Martini glasses are suitable for martinis, cosmopolitans, and blender drinks. Tumblers and straight-sided highball glasses are for mixed drinks and soft drinks.

dinnerware

Good-quality pieces with a simple design can work for any occasion, formal or casual. You can also mix in some heirloom dishes or colorful pieces to suit your personal style.

plates and bowls Plain white china is always appropriate and won't upstage the food you serve. For formal dinners, set each place with a charger—a large placeholder plate that serves as a liner under the first-course plate and is removed when the main course is served. Use shallow bowls for serving soup, pasta, and risotto, as well as some desserts.

flatware Good-quality, heavy flatware with a timeless design works for any occasion. Stainless-steel flatware is an acceptable option and is easy to clean. Sterling or silver plate dresses up the table, but plan on extra time for polishing and hand washing.

servingware

Ideally, your platters and bowls will match or complement your dinnerware. Stainless-steel serving utensils are a versatile choice as well. Accent with special heirloom pieces, antiques, or patterned servingware.

platters Use platters for serving meats, fish, appetizers, salads, cookies, and cheeses. For more dramatic presentations, use platters for serving, pasta, and risotto, and for unstructured desserts.

serving bowls Large, shallow serving bowls can be used for pastas, vegetable side dishes, and fruit salads. Use deeper bowls for mashed potatoes and other soft foods. A glass or wooden salad bowl will match any style.

utensils Be sure to have several large spoons handy for putting out with your servingware. You will also need a meat fork, a few serving forks, one or two cheese knives, and a spatula for baked dishes.

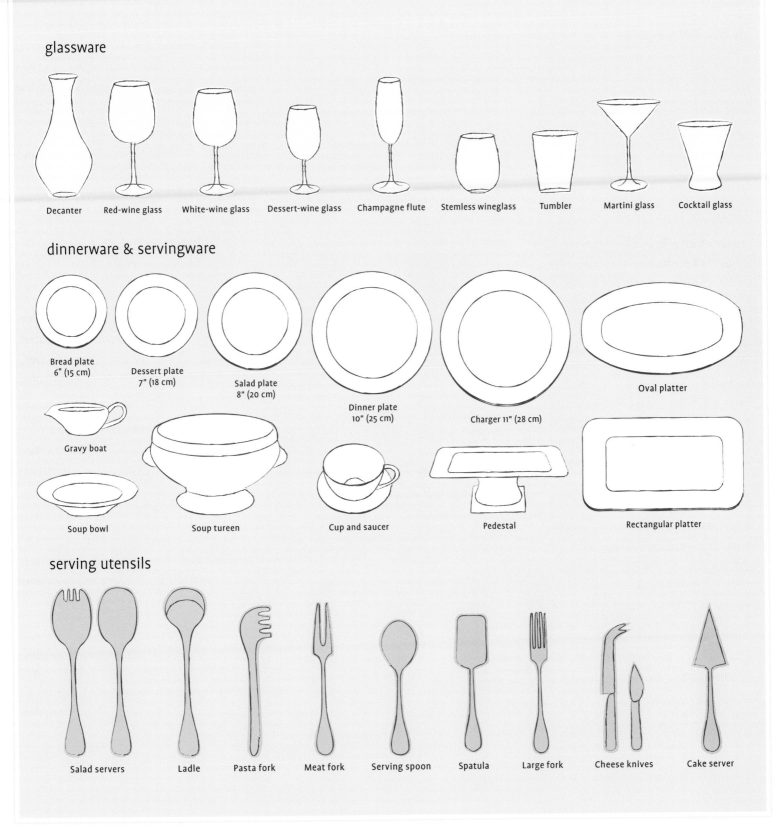

glassware

Decanter

Red-wine glass

White-wine glass

Dessert-wine glass

Champagne flute

Stemless wineglass

Tumbler

Martini glass

Cocktail glass

dinnerware & servingware

Bread plate
6" (15 cm)

Dessert plate
7" (18 cm)

Salad plate
8" (20 cm)

Dinner plate
10" (25 cm)

Charger 11" (28 cm)

Oval platter

Gravy boat

Soup bowl

Soup tureen

Cup and saucer

Pedestal

Rectangular platter

serving utensils

Salad servers

Ladle

Pasta fork

Meat fork

Serving spoon

Spatula

Large fork

Cheese knives

Cake server

formal setting

Here are the elements for a formal setting, which will vary according to your menu and the pieces that you own.

napkin A folded napkin is placed to the left of the forks, its folded side facing the plate, ready to be picked up and laid across the lap as a guest sits down.

bread plate with butter knife Set a small plate for bread just above the forks, and lay a small butter knife across it so it faces the left on a slight diagonal.

salad fork Forks are placed to the left of the plate. If salad will be served before the main course, set the salad fork in the outermost position; if after, place it to the right of the dinner fork.

dinner fork Used for the main course, this is the largest fork in the setting.

dessert fork Set nearest the dinner plate at the start of the meal, or brought out with the dessert course. If you do not own dessert forks, salad forks can be used.

charger Also known as the service plate, the charger is used in the initial place setting and remains as a liner under the first-course plate until the main course is served.

dinner plate This large plate is used for the main course and side dishes. Warm in a microwave or low oven just before serving.

salad plate This small plate can also be used for first courses and desserts. It is often chilled when used for serving salads or other first courses.

knife A sturdy table knife is set to the right of the plate, its blade facing inward. If you are serving steaks, chops, or roasted meat, you may use steak knives in place of table knives.

teaspoon Place a teaspoon to the right of the knife. Or, you can bring out the teaspoons at the same time you bring out the coffee and tea. If serving soup, place a soupspoon to the right of the teaspoon.

water glass Set a tumbler or goblet for water just above the knife. Fill water glasses just before the guests are seated.

wineglass To the right and slightly above the water glass, set the wineglass for the first wine being served (usually a white). For each additional wine you plan to pour, place another wineglass to the right of the previous one on a slight diagonal.

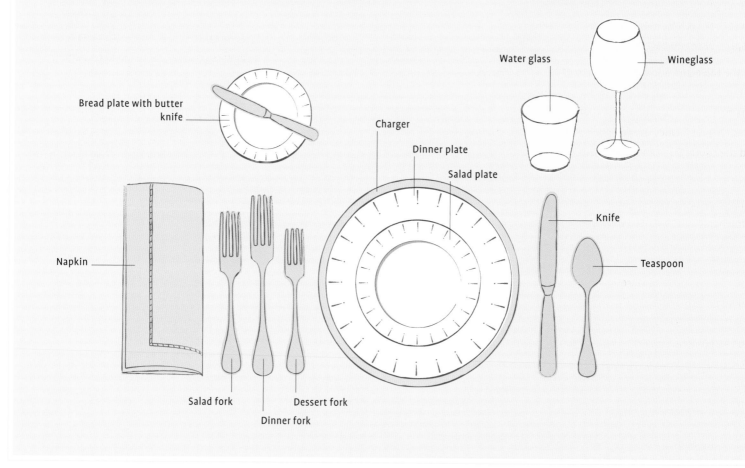

Bread plate with butter knife

Napkin

Salad fork

Dinner fork

Dessert fork

Charger

Dinner plate

Salad plate

Water glass

Wineglass

Knife

Teaspoon

setting a festive table

Even the most elegant holiday table should be more special than formal. In keeping with the menu and the occasion, make the table celebratory and memorable by adding little extravagances to delight your guests.

pitchers, punch bowls, and carafes Place pitchers of still and sparkling water on small liner plates on the table or sideboard. Use pitchers or a punch bowl for batch drinks. If you prefer, decant wine into a decanter or carafes before serving. An ice bucket is useful for chilling sparkling and white wine.

elements of the table Begin by making a seating chart. This is helpful because it relieves guests of the pressure of deciding where to sit. Allow about 2 feet (60 cm) of space between each setting.

Set the table and add a place card to each setting. You might also want to add a holiday ornament, a small gift, or other party favor for each guest. Once everything is in place, add the centerpiece and candles.

serving the meal Welcome guests with drinks and appetizers in the living room. Just before you invite them to the table, light the candles and fill the water glasses. The first course can be preset at each place, or passed around the table. For more intimate groups, you might want to bring the main course and side dishes to the head of the table, where you can compose plates and pass them to each guest. Or you can pass platters, standing to the left of guests, so that they can help themselves with their right hands.

Soup, salad, and dessert can be plated in the kitchen or served from the head of the table. Pour coffee and tea in the kitchen or from the sideboard, and then circulate as needed to refill cups.

clearing the table Always wait until everyone has finished before clearing. If the group is large, recruit someone in advance to help you. Clear dishes and flatware for each course, picking them up from the right and carrying only a few at a time. To save time, you can return from the kitchen with the plates for the next course to replace the ones you have just cleared. Before dessert, clear all the unused flatware, bread plates, salt and pepper cellars, and wineglasses that will no longer be used. Brush crumbs from the table with a crumber or folded napkin onto a small tray or plate. Reset the table with any flatware or glassware needed for dessert.

the holiday buffet

A buffet is the way to go for big holiday celebrations, from casual open houses and brunches to elegant dinners and cocktail parties. Choose a table or sideboard, and arrange your empty trays and platters on it in advance to be sure there will be room for everything. You might want to move the table away from the wall, so it is accessible from both sides. Use some footed platters of varying heights to add visual interest. Place dinner or appetizer plates at the end where the guests will start and napkins and flatware at the other end, so diners won't have to juggle them while serving

themselves. Arrange the flow of dishes so that cold ones come first, followed by hot items. Use trivets, warming trays, or chafing dishes as needed to protect the table and keep food hot. Make sure each dish has an appropriate serving utensil. Add a few holiday decorations, such as candles and greenery, that tie in with the table centerpiece. If you are serving Thanksgiving or Christmas dinner buffet style, you may want to display the whole turkey or ham, rather than a platter of sliced meat. You can then stand at the buffet and carve slices for each guest.

setting up the bar

Big holiday get-togethers, and especially cocktail parties, call for a drink station, which can be either self-service or tended. Select a sturdy table for the purpose or designate an area on the kitchen counter, near the sink. Spread a plastic tablecloth over the surface, and then cover it with a linen tablecloth or mats to absorb spills. Arrange ice, glassware, spirits, and garnishes in a logical flow for easy drink making. Be sure to leave ample workspace for mixing and measuring. Place an open bottle or two of red wine on the bar, and an open bottle of white and/or sparkling wine in an ice bucket. Near or under the bar, store backup bottles of red wine and a large ice tub with chilled wines, beer, and soft drinks. Set up trash receptacles or trays where guests can set plates, flatware, and glasses when they have finished using them. For large functions, you can turn the bar into a coffee and tea station as the party begins to wind down.

Ingredient Glossary

Apples Primarily a late-summer through autumn crop, apples are a favorite fruit of the holiday season. Tart green apples, often used in baking, include Granny Smith, an Australian variety, and pippin, green to yellow-green apples with a slightly tart taste. Sweet, red-blushed Northern Spy apples are also a good choice, as they hold their shape during cooking. Among the large, sweet varieties are the slightly tart Rome Beauty, ideal for baking or eating raw, and the red-and-green McIntosh, which is also good raw and cooked.

Calvados Also known as applejack, Calvados is a dry brandy made from apples in the Normandy region of France. Its distinctive flavor makes it an ideal base for such holiday drinks as Apple Cider Cocktail (page 86).

Campari Red-hued Campari adds a festive coloring to many cocktails. Created in 1867 in Milan, Italy, it is flavored with an assortment of herbs, fruits, spices, and other botanicals and is traditionally drunk as an aperitif. Because of its distinctive bitterness, it is usually combined with orange or grapefruit juice or a splash of soda.

Chocolate Made from the tropical cacao bean, chocolate is used in many holiday recipes, from cakes and cookies to candies and other confections. Always purchase the best-quality chocolate you can afford. Many cooks prefer European chocolate, but nowadays several excellent artisanal brands are marketed by U.S. and South American manufacturers. Here are the primary types of chocolate:

Bittersweet A lightly sweetened eating or baking chocolate with a full, rich flavor. Look for bittersweet chocolate that contains at least 61 percent cacao (percentage by weight of cacao bean, with the balance primarily sugar). The higher the percentage, the more bitter the taste will be.

Milk This popular eating chocolate is made from cocoa butter, milk powder, and sugar.

Semisweet Also known as plain chocolate, this eating or baking chocolate is slightly sweeter than bittersweet, for which it may be substituted. The cacao percentage can be as low as 30 percent.

White A chocolate-like product made by combining cocoa butter, sugar, milk powder, and sometimes vanilla extract. Check labels to be sure that the white chocolate you buy is made exclusively with cocoa butter, and without the addition of coconut oil or vegetable shortening.

Cider Hot apple cider is a popular drink during the cold winter months, especially at holiday parties. Traditionally made by blending the juice from a variety of apples, both sweet and tart, apple cider can be drunk plain or with spices added, as in Hot Mulled Cider (page 74).

Citrus Oranges and lemons are just two of the many types of citrus fruits abundant during the cold-weather months. All of them are favorite additions to holiday dishes, from appetizers to mains to desserts.

Blood oranges Oranges that have a distinctive red flesh and juice and a flavor reminiscent of berries. They can be used alongside or in place of navel oranges.

Clementines These small, loose-skinned mandarin oranges have a glossy, deep orange rind and sweet, red-orange flesh with few or no seeds. Clementines can be sweet or tart.

Grapefruit A cross between an orange and a pomelo. The grapefruit has a tart, refreshing flavor and an abundance of juice. Depending on the variety, the pulp ranges from white to pale pink to ruby red.

Limes Slightly smaller and more delicate than lemons, limes are pleasantly tart with just a hint of sweetness. They can be used in place of lemons in almost any recipe.

Meyer lemons Slightly smaller, sweeter, and more fragrant than a regular Eureka or Lisbon lemon, the popular Meyer also has looser skin, making it easier to handle.

Navel oranges The most widely available type of orange. Navel oranges are sweet, easy to peel, and almost always seedless, making them ideal for juicing and eating out of hand.

Tangerines These members of the mandarin orange group have deeper-colored skins than other mandarins and a more sweet-sour taste than most regular oranges.

Confections The term commonly used for a wide variety of candies, from truffles and caramels to nougats—treats popular to both make and give away during the holiday season.

Cookies Dropped, rolled and cut out, piped, pressed—all types of cookies are baked and eaten during the holidays. They are fun to make and decorate and are easily packed into pretty boxes or tins for gift giving. Or, you can host friends and family at a traditional holiday cookie exchange.

Crab A much-relished delicacy, crab is a holiday tradition on many family tables. The big, meat-packed Dungeness is pulled from Pacific waters, while the smaller, mild-flavored blue crab (named for its blue claws) is abundant on the Atlantic and Gulf coasts.

Cranberries Native to North America, the cranberry is an integral part of many holiday dishes, from cranberry relish served with Thanksgiving turkey to cranberry pie. The berries are harvested throughout the fall, with most of the crop finding its way to commercial food processors for sauce and juice. Cranberries are too tart to eat raw on their own but lend themselves to savory and sweet preparations, marrying nicely with other fruits, such as apples and pears, and with nuts and grains. Fresh cranberries should be plump and firm and range from deep scarlet to light red. Both fresh and frozen whole cranberries are packaged in plastic bags, rather than sold loose. Refrigerate the berries for up to 1 month, or freeze them for up to 10 months.

Dates Sweet, sticky, and splendid, dates grow in heavy profusion on towering date palms that flourish in the desert climates of North Africa, the Middle East, and southern California. Dates are available year-round, although their peak season is from October through January, making them favorite holiday treats. Medjool, Khadrawy, and Halawy are common varieties.

Eggnog An indispensable component of any holiday gathering, this thick, creamy beverage can be served as a nonalcoholic drink or with the addition of a spirit, such as brandy. Recipes vary, but the most common include egg yolks, sugar, milk, cream, and nutmeg.

Figs Figs are eaten both fresh and dried, and at holiday time, the dried fruits are popular additions to breads and cakes and are often accompaniments to a cheese course.

Ginger The brown, gnarled, knobby appearance of fresh ginger belies its refreshing and slightly sweet flavor. It also packs a fair amount of spiciness. Although mistakenly called a root, ginger is actually a rhizome, or underground stem. Fresh ginger, usually peeled and sliced, minced, or grated, adds a bright note of flavor to rich dishes. Crystallized ginger, candied in sugar syrup and then coated with granulated sugar, adds sweet-spicy flavor to dessert fillings, cake batters, ice cream, or fruit salad. Ground dried ginger adds a delightful fragrance and flavor to many breads, cookies, and cakes.

Gingerbread A signature treat of the Christmas season, gingerbread turns up in a trio of forms: a crisp or soft cookie that is often decorated; a rich, dark cake; and, of course, as the building material for the edible holiday house.

Horseradish A thick, gnarled root with a refreshing, spicy bite, horseradish perks up savory dishes, such as Beef Crostini with Horseradish and Watercress (page 112).

Lemon Verbena A native of South America, lemon verbena has long, narrow leaves and a robust, fruity lemon scent. It can be used fresh or dried.

Lillet An herb-infused wine from the Bordeaux region of France of the same name, Lillet is typically served over ice, either on its own or with a splash of sparkling water and enjoyed as an apéritif. It comes in a red and white version, though white is the more common.

Molasses A by-product of sugar refinement, a process that requires repeated boiling of cane syrup, molasses—a thick, sweet syrup—comes in three basic types: light, dark, and blackstrap. It is used to top breakfast dishes, flavor sauces, and sweeten baked goods, such as Chewy Ginger-Molasses Cookies (page 260).

Nuts Among the holiday kitchen's most versatile ingredients, nuts can be packaged and given as gifts, such as Spiced Rosemary Nuts (page 268), or added to both savory dishes and sweets.

Almonds The meat found inside the pit of a dry fruit related to peaches, the almond is delicate and fragrant. It has a pointed, oval shape and a smooth texture that lends itself well to many elegant presentations as well as recipes.

Peanuts Not really a nut at all, but rather a type of legume that grows underground, peanuts are seeds nestled inside waffle-veined pods that become thin and brittle when dried.

Pecans These delicately flavored nuts are harvested in October and November, just in time for the holidays. They have two deeply crinkled lobes of nutmeat, much like their relative, the walnut, and a smooth, oval shell that breaks easily.

Pistachios The pistachio has a creamy tan, thin, hard round shell. As the nuts ripen, their shells crack to reveal bright green kernels. Pistachios are a popular addition to many holiday desserts and salads.

Walnuts The furrowed, double-lobed nutmeat of the walnut has a rich, assertive flavor. The most common variety is the English walnut, also known as Persian walnut, which has a light brown shell that cracks easily.

Orange Blossom Water Made by distilling the essential oils of orange blossoms, this highly fragrant water is used in ice creams, baked goods, and syrups. Look for it in Middle Eastern stores and specialty-foods markets.

Oysters Few combinations are as perfect for a celebration as fresh shucked oysters and Champagne. Oysters can also star in soups, stews, and stuffings. Always buy them from a reputable fishmonger who can vouch that they come from unpolluted waters. Fresh live oysters in the shell have a mild, sweet smell. Their shells should be closed tightly and the oysters should feel heavy in your hand.

Parsnips A relative of the carrot, this ivory-colored root closely resembles its brighter, more familiar cousin. Parsnips have a slightly sweet flavor and a tough, starchy texture that softens with cooking. They can be prepared in almost any way that potatoes or carrots are.

Pears This autumn fruit is the hallmark of many holiday desserts. Thousands of different pear varieties exist, including the yellow-tinged Anjou, which works well in salads; the all-purpose Bartlett (also known as the Williams'); the versatile, long-necked Bosc, excellent for baking and poaching; and the buttery-fleshed Comice, another good baker.

Peppermint The sweet, hot flavor of peppermint is highlighted in many holiday treats from cocktails to cookies, such as peppermint liqueur-laced Mojito Peppermint Fizz (page 70) and rich, decadent Chocolate-Peppermint Crinkles (page 264).

Pomegranate This deep red winter fruit has a tough, leathery skin that splits open to reveal an abundance of jewel-toned seeds. Its juice adds color and flavor to cocktails and its seeds deliver sparkle and crunch to drinks, salads, and other dishes. Select thin-skinned fruits that feel heavy in your hand, and store at room temperature for 3 to 5 days, or in a plastic bag in the refrigerator for up to 3 weeks.

Pumpkin A popular cold-weather member of the gourd family, pumpkins range in color from pale ivory to a deep red-tinged orange. Seek out small, sweet varieties, such as Sugar Pie, Baby Bear, or Cheese pumpkins for cooking and baking. There are also many excellent brands of canned pumpkin purée, all of which offering convenience to busy cooks.

Rosemary Used fresh or dried, this Mediterranean herb has a pungent flavor that complements meats and poultry. It is also a good addition to holiday stuffings and to potato and other vegetable dishes.

Rum Distilled from sugarcane juice or molasses, this Caribbean liquor comes in a variety of shades, including light, also called white or silver; amber, also known as gold; and dark, with the deep-colored types the most strongly flavored. With its slightly sweet taste, rum is enjoyed straight, over the rocks, or in drinks, such as Hot Rum Coffee (page 74) and Boston Eggnog with Cardamom (page 86).

Sea Salt Additive free and naturally evaporated, sea salt is available in coarse or fine grains shaped like flaky pyramids. As a result, it adheres better to foods and dissolves more quickly than table salt. Most sea salt comes from France, England, or the United States, with grayish ivory *fleur de sel* from Brittany among the most prized.

Smoked Salmon This favorite delicacy is typically a fillet that is first cured in salt and then either hot or cold smoked. Cold-smoked salmon is commonly known as lox, but both types are versatile and delicious with eggs or with bagels and cream cheese for breakfast or as an ingredient in holiday canapés or other hors d'oeuvres.

Spices Many different spices add enticing flavors to both savory and sweet dishes.

Cardamom This sweet, exotic-tasting spice is used mainly in baking. Its small, round seeds are best purchased whole, then ground with a spice grinder or a mortar and pestle as needed.

Cinnamon The aromatic bark of a type of evergreen tree, cinnamon is sold as whole dried strips—cinnamon sticks—or ground.

Nutmeg The hard pit of the fruit of the nutmeg tree. This popular baking spice can be bought already ground or, for fresher flavor, whole and then grated as needed.

Turkey Benjamin Franklin wanted to make the turkey the national bird of the United Sates, and it unofficially becomes that every year at Thanksgiving, when Americans consume this bird in incredible numbers. Turkey is nearly as popular at Christmas and is also eaten throughout the year, often as a low-fat substitute for red meat. For the best taste, choose a fresh bird that was raised free-range and fed organic grain. Although these birds are more expensive, they have more flavor than their factory-farm counterparts. Order them from reputable butchers or good-quality grocery stores.

Yorkshire Pudding Named for England's northern country of Yorkshire, this savory dish is essentially a cooked batter made of eggs, flour, and milk and is similar to the American popover. Originally, Yorkshire pudding was baked below a roast so it could catch the drippings of the meat to flavor it. Nowadays, it is baked separately and served with gravy drizzled on top.

Index

A

Almonds
Almond Pound Cake with Cherry Glaze, 206
Citrus Salad with Mint and Marcona Almonds, 134
Israeli Couscous with Squash, Feta, and Almonds, 140

Antipasto platters, 104

Apple cider
Apple Cider Cocktail, 86
Apple-Ginger Fizz, 78
Baked Ham with Spiced Cider Glaze, 166
Cider-Shallot Pan Gravy, 161
Hot Mulled Cider, 74

Apples
Apple Tarte Tatin, 224
Baked Goat Cheese with Honey and Apples, 103
Latticed Apple Pie, 209
Sausage, Apple, and Thyme Stuffing, 163
Sausages with Sautéed Apples and Onions, 236
Watercress Salad with Apple, Celery, and Blue Cheese, 134

Avocado, Butter Lettuce Salad with Shrimp and, 137

B

Beans
Green Beans with Bacon and Onion Vinaigrette, 185
White Bean Soup with Rosemary, 121

Beef
Beef Crostini with Horseradish and Watercress, 112
Filet Mignon Skewers with Balsamic Reduction, 117
Filet Mignon with Red Currant and Wine Sauce, 169
Rosemary Rib Roast with Yorkshire Pudding, 171

Beets, Roasted, Spinach Salad with Orange and, 135

Bell peppers
Cheddar and Roasted Red Pepper Dip, 98
Frittata with Spinach, Roasted Red Peppers, and Gruyère, 233
Turkey Breast with Chorizo, Oregano, and Peppers, 157

Biscotti, Chocolate Cranberry-Pistachio, 263

Biscuits, Maple-Thyme, 191

Blueberries
Blueberry Syrup, 267
Buttermilk-Blueberry Scone Bites, 240

Boston Eggnog with Cardamom, 86

Bourbon
Chapel Hill Cocktail, 81

Brandy
Apple Cider Cocktail, 86
Boston Eggnog with Cardamom, 86

Bread. See also Croutons; Stuffing
Assorted Panini Bites, 114
Beef Crostini with Horseradish and Watercress, 112
Buttermilk-Blueberry Scone Bites, 240
Classic Dinner Rolls, 193
Cranberry Cornmeal Muffins, 241
Fig and Walnut Quick Bread, 261
Maple-Thyme Biscuits, 191
Olive Bread, 194
Persimmon Bread Pudding, 214
Rosemary Popovers, 192

Brittle, Pistachio, 250

Broccoli Rabe with Lemon Zest, 185

Brunches, 9

Brussels Sprouts with Shallots and Parmesan, 186

Buffets, 10, 20, 277

Buttermilk-Blueberry Scone Bites, 240

C

Cakes
Almond Pound Cake with Cherry Glaze, 206
Cinnamon Coffee Bundt Cake, 242
decorating, 222
Gingerbread Bundt Cake, 215
Pumpkin-Ginger Cheesecake, 218
Rich Chocolate Brownie Cake, 221

Camparini, 85

Canapés, Smoked Salmon, with Caviar, 111

Candles, 13, 32–33, 38, 47, 52, 67

Cardamom Crème Brûlée, 202

Caramel Sea Salt Triffles, 258

Carrots and Parsnips, Glazed, with Sherry, 177

Cauliflower Gratin, 182

Celery Root and Potatoes, Mashed, 178

Centerpieces, 32–35, 46–49, 60–63

Champagne
French 75 Champagne Cocktail, 73
Grapefruit Champagne Punch, 73

Cheese
antipasto platters, 104
Artisanal-Cheese Fondue, 102
Baked Goat Cheese with Honey and Apples, 103
Cheddar and Roasted Red Pepper Dip, 98
Cheese Straws with Sesame Seeds, 94
Dates Stuffed with Fontina and Hazelnuts, 99
Endive with Gorgonzola, Pear, and Walnuts, 100
Frittata with Spinach, Roasted Red Peppers, and Gruyère, 233
Israeli Couscous with Squash, Feta, and Almonds, 140
Marinated Goat Cheese, 273
matching wine and, 89
Mixed Greens and Fennel with Ricotta Salata, 130
Pumpkin-Ginger Cheesecake, 218
Radicchio Salad with Pears, Walnuts, and Goat Cheese, 133
Ricotta-Stuffed Cherry Tomatoes, 100
Scrambled Eggs with Mushrooms, Cheddar and Pancetta, 235
serving, 198
Soufflé Ricotta Pancakes with Orange Maple Syrup, 238
Sweet Potato Soup with Cheddar, and Caviar Croutons, 129
Watercress Salad with Apple, Celery, and Blue Cheese, 134
and wine gathering, 21

Cherry Glaze, 206

Chex-and-Nut Mix, Three-Spice, 98

Chicken, Tarragon-Stuffed, with Pan Gravy, 156

Chicory and Smoked Trout Salad, 138

Chile Dipping Sauce, 147

Chocolate
    Caramel Sea Salt Truffles, 258
    Chocolate Cranberry-Pistachio Biscotti, 263
    Chocolate Ganache Filling, 257
    Chocolate-Marshmallow Fudge, 248
    Chocolate-Pecan Crostata, 217
    Chocolate-Peppermint Crinkles, 264
    Chocolate Pots de Crème, 204
    Ice Cream Truffles, 228
    purchasing, 221
    Rich Chocolate Brownie Cake, 221
    shavings, 222

Chowder, Classic Clam, 128

Christmas celebrations
    centerpiece for, 46–49
    kitchen preparation for, 45
    lighting for, 52
    menus for, 24
    planning for, 43, 44, 45
    serving, 44, 45
    setting table for, 44, 45, 49

Cinnamon
    Cinnamon Coffee Bundt Cake, 242
    Cinnamon Ice Cream, 225
    Cinnamon-Spice Whipped Cream, 207

Citrus fruits. See also individual fruits
    Blood Orange Granita, 227
    Blood Orange Marmalade, 270
    Candied Grapefruit Peel, 266
    Citrus Salad with Mint and Marcona Almonds, 134
    Clementine-Mint Sparkler, 77
    Grapefruit Compote with Fresh Mint, 232
    grilled, as garnish, 155
    ice cubes with, 81
    Spincach Salad with Orange and Roasted Beets, 135
    Warm Citrus Olives, 103

Clam Chowder, Classic, 128

Clementine-Mint Sparkler, 77

Cocktail parties, 9, 10, 23, 25

Coconut Macaroons, 253

Cod Fillets, True, with Shallot and Meyer Lemon Sauce, 148

Coffee, Hot Rum, 74

Compote, Grapefruit, with Fresh Mint, 232

Cookies
    Chewy Ginger-Molasses Cookies, 260
    Chocolate Cranberry-Pistachio Biscotti, 263
    Chocolate-Peppermint Crinkles, 264
    Coconut Macaroons, 253
    decorating, 254
    Lemon Zest Shortbread, 251
    as party favors, 64
    Sugar Cookies, 256

Cosmopolitan, Ginger, 70

Couscous, Israeli, with Squash, Feta, and Almonds, 140

Crab
    Crab Soufflé, 145
    Cucumbers with Pickled Ginger and Crab, 108
    Fresh Cracked Crab with Chile Dipping Sauce, 147

Crackers, Homemade, 124

Cranberries
    Chocolate Cranberry-Pistachio Biscotti, 263
    Cranberry and Pear Crisp, 220
    Cranberry Cornmeal Muffins, 241
    Cranberry-Lime Punch, 81
    Ginger Cosmopolitan, 70
    Gingered Cranberries, 188
    Mushroom Stuffing with Herbs and Cranberries, 160

Crème Anglaise, 207

Crème Brûlée, Cardamom, 202

Crème fraîche
    Ginger Crème Fraîche, 120
    as soup topping, 122

Crisp, Cranberry and Pear, 220

Crostata, Chocolate-Pecan, 217

Crostini, Beef, with Horseradish and Watercress, 112

Croutons
    Cheddar and Caviar Croutons, 129
    Rosemary Croutons, 125
    as soup topping, 122

Cucumbers with Pickled Ginger and Crab, 108

D

Dates Stuffed with Fontina and Hazelnuts, 99

Decorating, 13

Dinnerware, 274, 275

Dips
    Caramelized Onion and Sour Cream Dip, 97
    Cheddar and Roasted Red Pepper Dip, 98

Drinks. See also Wine
    Apple Cider Cocktail, 86
    Apple-Ginger Fizz, 78
    Boston Eggnog with Cardamom, 86
    Camparini, 85
    Chapel Hill Cocktail, 81
    Clementine-Mint Sparkler, 77
    Cranberry-Lime Punch, 81
    estimating quantities of, 11
    French 75 Champagne Cocktail, 73
    Ginger Cosmopolitan, 70
    Grapefruit Champagne Punch, 73
    Hot Mulled Cider, 74
    Hot Rum Coffee, 74
    Lemon Verbena Drop with Thyme, 82
    Lillet Cocktail, 85
    Mojito Peppermint Fizz, 70
    Pomegranate Frost, 78
    Ruby Red Grapefruit Martini, 82
    station for, 277
    Winter Swizzle, 77

E

Eggs
    Boston Eggnog with Cardamom, 86
    Crab Soufflé, 145
    Frittata with Spinach, Roasted Red Peppers, and Gruyère, 233
    Scrambled Eggs with Mushrooms, Cheddar, and Pancetta, 235

Endive with Gorgonzola, Pear, and Walnuts, 100

Escarole
    Mixed Greens and Fennel with Ricotta Salata, 130
    Spicy Braised Escarole, 187

F

Family-style service, 10

Fennel
  Mixed Greens and Fennel with Ricotta Salata, 130
  Olive and Fennel Relish, 188
  Sautéed Fennel and Garlic, 179

Fig and Walnut Quick Bread, 261

Fish
  Smoked Salmon Canapés with Caviar, 111
  Smoked Salmon Fillet with Toppings, 151
  Smoked Trout and Chicory Salad, 138
  True Cod Fillets with Shallot and Meyer Lemon Sauce, 148

Flowers, 13, 35, 46, 49, 60, 63

Fondue
  Artisanal-Cheese Fondue, 102

Formal dinner parties, 9, 10, 276

French 75 Champagne Cocktail, 73

Frittata with Spinach, Roasted Red Peppers, and Gruyère, 233

Fudge, Chocolate-Marshmallow, 248

G

Gifts
  ideas for, 248–73
  packaging, 247

Gin
  French 75 Champagne Cocktail, 73
  Lillet Cocktail, 85

Ginger
  Chewy Ginger-Molasses Cookies, 260
  Cucumbers with Pickled Ginger and Crab, 108
  Gingerbread Bundt Cake, 215
  Ginger Cosmopolitan, 70
  Ginger Crème Fraîche, 120
  Gingered Cranberries, 188
  Ginger Mignonette, 92
  Pumpkin-Ginger Cheeseacake, 218

Glassware, 274, 275

H

Ham
  Assorted Panini Bites, 114
  Baked Ham with Spiced Cider Glaze, 166

Hazelnuts, Dates Stuffed with Fontina and, 99

Granita, Blood Orange, 227

Grapefruit
  Camparini, 85
  Candied Grapefruit Peel, 266
  Citrus Salad with Mint and Marcona Almonds, 134
  Grapefruit Champagne Punch, 73
  Grapefruit Compote with Fresh Mint, 232
  Ruby Red Grapefruit Martini, 82
  Winter Swizzle, 77

Gravy
  Cider-Shallot Pan Gravy, 161
  Pan Gravy, 156

Greens, Mixed, and Fennel with Ricotta Salata, 130

I

Ice cream
  Cinnamon Ice Cream, 225
  Ice Cream Truffles, 228
  sandwiches, 225

Icing, Royal, 257

Invitations, 10

L

Lamb
  Grilled Lamb Chops with Olive-Mint Tapenade, 113
  Rack of Lamb with Garlic and Fresh Herbs, 165

Leek Soup with Pancetta and Bread Crumbs, 127

Lemons
  as centerpiece, 63
  Lemon Zest Shortbread, 251
  Preserved Lemons, 271
  Sautéed Scallops with Meyer Lemon Relish, 107

Lemon Verbena Drop with Thyme, 82

Lighting, 13, 38, 52, 67

Lillet Cocktail, 85

Linens, 274

M

Macadamia-Caramel Tart, 203

Macaroons, Coconut, 253

Maple syrup
  Maple Glaze, 162
  Maple-Thyme Biscuits, 191
  Orange Maple Syrup, 238

Marmalade, Blood Orange, 270

Marshmallow-Chocolate Fudge, 248

Martini, Ruby Red Grapefruit, 82

Menus, 10, 18–25

Mojito Peppermint Fizz, 70

Muffins, Cranberry Cornmeal, 241

Mushrooms
  Mushroom Stuffing with Herbs and Cranberries, 160
  Risotto with Porcini Mushrooms, 144
  Scrambled Eggs with Mushrooms, Cheddar, and Pancetta, 235
  Wild Rice Salad, 139
  Wild Rice with Mushrooms and Winter Squash, 18

N

New Year's celebrations
  centerpiece for, 60–61
  kitchen preparation for, 59
  lighting for, 67
  menus for, 25
  planning for, 57, 58, 59
  serving, 58, 59
  setting the scene for, 58, 59, 63

Nutmeg Whipped Cream, 215

Nuts. See also individual nuts

Chocolate-Pecan Crostata, 217
Ice Cream Truffles, 228
Macadamia-Caramel Tart, 203
Spiced Rosemary Nuts, 268

O

Olives
Olive and Fennel Relish, 188
Olive Bread, 194
Olive-Mint Tapenade, 113
Warm Citrus Olives, 103

Onions
Caramelized Onion and Sour Cream
Dip, 97
Sausages with Sautéed Apples and
Onions, 236

Open houses, 9, 10, 25

Oranges
Blood Orange Granita, 227
Blood Orange Marmalade, 270
Citrus Salad with Mint and Marcona
Almonds, 134
Grapefruit Champagne Punch, 73
Orange Maple Syrup, 238
Spinach Salad with Orange and Roasted
Beets, 135

Oysters, 92

P

Pancakes, Soufflé Ricotta, with Orange
Maple Syrup, 238

Pan Gravy, 156

Panini Bites, Assorted, 114

Parsnips and Carrots, Glazed, with
Sherry, 177

Pasta, matching wine and, 89

Pears
as centerpiece, 49
Cranberry and Pear Crisp, 220
Endive with Gorgonzola, Pear, and
Walnuts, 100

Poached Pears in Red Wine, 201
Radicchio Salad with Pears, Walnuts, and
Goat Cheese, 133

Pecans
Chocolate-Pecan Crostata, 217
Cinnamon Coffee Bundt Cake, 242

Persimmons
as centerpiece, 35
Persimmon Bread Pudding, 214

Pies
Latticed Apple Pie, 209
Pumpkin Pie with Walnut Crust, 210
seasonal toppings for, 213

Pinzimonio, 104

Pistachios
Chocolate Cranberry-Pistachio Biscotti, 263
Pistachio Brittle, 250
Three-Spice Chex-and-Nut Mix, 98

Place cards, 36, 45, 51, 67

Pomegranates
as garnish, 13
ice cubes with, 81
place cards with, 51
Pomegranate Frost, 78

Popovers, Rosemary, 192

Pork. See also Ham; Sausage
Roast Pork Loin with Salt-and-Fennel Rub, 168

Potatoes
Classic Clam Chowder, 128
Mashed Potatoes and Celery Root, 178
Potato Gratin Rounds with Thyme, 174
Twice-Cooked Potatoes with Fresh Herbs, 237

Pots de Crème, Chocolate, 204

Pudding, Persimmon Bread, 214

Pumpkin
as place cards, 36
Pumpkin-Ginger Cheesecake, 218
Pumpkin Pie with Walnut Crust, 210

Punch
Cranberry-Lime Punch, 81
Grapefruit Champagne Punch, 73

R

Radicchio Salad with Pears, Walnuts, and
Goat Cheese, 133

Relish, Olive and Fennel, 188

Restaurant-style service, 10

Risotto with Porcini Mushrooms, 144

Rolls, Classic Dinner, 193

Root Vegetable Purée, 175

Rosemary
Rosemary Croutons, 125
Rosemary Nuts, Spiced, 268
Rosemary Popovers, 192
Rosemary Rib Roast with Yorkshire
Pudding, 171

Royal Icing, 257

Rum
Boston Eggnog with Cardamom, 86
Hot Rum Coffee, 74
Mojito Peppermint Fizz, 70

S

Salads
Butter Lettuce Salad with Avocado and Shrimp, 137
Citrus Salad with Mint and Marcona Almonds, 134
Israeli Couscous with Squash, Feta, and
Almonds, 140
Mixed Greens and Fennel with Ricotta Salata, 130
Radicchio Salad with Pears, Walnuts, and
Goat Cheese, 133
Smoked Trout and Chicory Salad, 138
Spinach Salad with Orange and Roasted
Beets, 135
Watercress Salad with Apple, Celery, and
Blue Cheese, 134
Wild Rice Salad, 139

Salmon
Smoked Salmon Canapés with Caviar, 111
Smoked Salmon Fillet with Toppings, 151

Sauces
Chile Dipping Sauce, 147
Crème Anglaise, 207

Ginger Mignonette, 92

Sherry Mignonette, 92

Sausage

Sausage, Apple, and Thyme Stuffing, 163

Sausages with Sautéed Apples and Onions, 236

Turkey Breast with Bacon, Oregano, and Peppers, 157

Scallops, Sautéed, with Meyer Lemon Relish, 107

Scone Bites, Buttermilk-Blueberry, 240

Servingware, 274, 275

Sesame Seeds, Cheese Straws with, 94

Sherry Mignonette, 92

Shortbread, Lemon Zest, 251

Shrimp, Butter Lettuce Salad with Avocado and, 137

Skewers, Filet Mignon, with Balsamic Reduction, 117

Soufflé, Crab, 145

Soufflé Ricotta Pancakes with Orange Maple Syrup, 238

Soups

Butternut Squash Soup with Ginger Crème Fraîche, 120

Classic Clam Chowder, 128

Leek Soup with Pancetta and Bread Crumbs, 127

Sweet Potato Soup with Cheddar and Caviar Croutons, 129

White Bean Soup with Rosemary, 121

Spinach

Frittata with Spinach, Roasted Red Peppers, and Gruyère, 233

Sautéed Scallops with Meyer Lemon Relish, 107

Spinach Salad with Orange and Roasted Beets, 135

Squash

Butternut Squash Soup with Ginger Crème Fraîche, 120

Israeli Couscous with Squash, Feta, and Almonds, 140

Roasted Squash with Maple Syrup and Sage Cream, 180

Wild Rice with Mushrooms and Winter Squash, 183

Stuffing

Mushroom Stuffing with Herbs and Cranberries, 160

Sausage, Apple, and Thyme Stuffing, 163

Sugar Cookies, 256

Sweet potatoes

Crunchy Sweet Potato Chips, 97

Sweet Potato Soup with Cheddar and Caviar Croutons, 129

Syrup, Blueberry, 267

T

Table, setting, 13, 29–31, 36, 44, 45, 49, 274–77

Tapenade, Olive-Mint, 113

Tarragon-Stuffed Chicken with Pan Gravy, 156

Tarts

Apple Tarte Tatin, 224

Chocolate-Pecan Crostata, 217

Macadamia-Caramel Tart, 203

Thanksgiving dinner

centerpiece for, 32–35

kitchen preparation for, 31

lighting for, 38

menus for, 18–19

planning for, 16, 29, 30

serving, 30, 31

setting table for, 29, 30, 31, 36

Tomatoes, Ricotta-Stuffed Cherry, 100

Triple sec

Chapel Hill Cocktail, 81

Trout, Smoked, and Chicory Salad, 138

Truffles

Caramel Sea Salt Truffles, 258

Ice Cream Truffles, 228

Turkey

Assorted Panini Bites, 114

garnishing, 155

Grilled Turkey with Maple Glaze, 162–63

leftover, 163

preparing, 152

Roast Turkey Seasoned with Sage, 158

Turkey Breast with Chorizo, Oregano, and Peppers, 157

V

Vermouth

Camparini, 85

Vodka

Ginger Cosmopolitan, 70

infused, 82

Lemon Verbena Drop with Thyme, 82

Ruby Red Grapefruit Martini, 82

W

Walnuts

Chocolate-Marshmallow Fudge, 248

Cinnamon Coffee Bundt Cake, 242

Endive with Gorgonzola, Pear, and Walnuts, 100

Fig and Walnut Quick Bread, 261

Pumpkin-Ginger Cheesecake, 218

Pumpkin Pie with Walnut Crust, 210

Radicchio Salad with Pears, Walnuts, and Goat Cheese, 133

Sausage, Apple, and Thyme Stuffing, 163

Watercress

Beef Crostini with Horseradish and Watercress, 112

Watercress Salad with Apple, Celery, and Blue Cheese, 134

Whipped cream

Cinnamon-Spice Whipped Cream, 207

Nutmeg Whipped Cream, 215

Wild rice

Wild Rice Salad, 139

Wild Rice with Mushrooms and Winter Squash, 183

Wine. See also Champagne

and cheese gathering, 21

matching food and, 89

serving, 88

splits, as party favors, 64

Winter Swizzle, 77

Y

Yorkshire Pudding, 171

Acknowledgments

WELDON OWEN wishes to thank the following individuals for their kind assistance:
Austin and Cary Adriatico; Birdman Inc.; Betsy and Noel Borg; Carrie Bradley; Audrey Chandler;
Peter Cieply; Brennie and Catherine Dale; Ben Davidson; Ken Della Penta; Alex and Max Diaz;
Judith Dunham; Holly Hogan; Jenny Koehler; Gabriel, Jeremy, and Laura Leary; Renée Myers;
Lesli Neilson; Julia Nelson; Phil Paulick; Amy Roediger; John and Susie Rosenberg; Sharon Silva;
Shannon and Matt Violante; Kate Washingon; and Barbara and John Witt.

GEORGEANNE BRENNAN would like to thank her husband, Jim, who is her best sampler.

LAUREN HUNTER would like to thank the entire creative team at Weldon Owen, Emma
and Amy especially; her assistants Daniele and Lori; Jamie and Lillian for the gorgeous food
styling; Joe Keller for his beautiful photography, and the following stores for inspiration
and props: Bae, Britex Fabrics, Chelsea Antiques, Columbine, Dandelion, Ellington & French,
Heath Ceramics, I Leoni, Nancy Koltes at Home, Paper Source, Sienna Antiques, Simon Pearce,
Sue Fisher King, Summer Cottage Antiques, The Gardener, Trove, and Tuscan Gardens.

OXMOOR HOUSE

Oxmoor House books are distributed by Sunset Books

80 Willow Road, Menlo Park, CA 94025

Telephone: 650 324 1532

VP and Associate Publisher Jim Childs

Director of Sales Brad Moses

Oxmoor House and Sunset Books are divisions
of Southern Progress Corporation

A WELDON OWEN PRODUCTION

First printed in 2007

Printed in China

Printed by Midas Printing Limited

10 9 8 7 6 5 4 3 2 1

Library of Congress Cataloging-in-Publication Data is available.

ISBN-13: 978-0-8487-3193-9

ISBN-10: 0-8487-3193-X

Jacket Images

Front cover: Rich Chocolate Brownie Cake (page 221).

Back cover: French 75 Champagne Cocktail and Grapefruit
Champagne Punch (page 73); Roast Turkey Seasoned with
Sage (page 158), Cider-Shallot Pan Gravy (page 161), Gingered
Cranberries (page 188), Mashed Potatoes with Celery Root
(page 178), and Green Beans with Bacon and Onion
Vinaigrette (page 185); Candied Grapefruit Peel (page 266).

THE ENTERTAINING SERIES

Conceived and produced by Weldon Owen Inc.

814 Montgomery Street, San Francisco, CA 94133

Telephone: 415 291 0100 Fax: 415 291 8841

In Collaboration with Williams-Sonoma, Inc.

3250 Van Ness Avenue, San Francisco, CA 94109

WILLIAMS-SONOMA, INC.

Founder & Vice-Chairman Chuck Williams

WELDON OWEN INC.

CEO, Weldon Owen Group John Owen

CEO and President, Weldon Owen Inc. Terry Newell

CFO, Weldon Owen Group Simon Fraser

VP, Sales and New Business Development Amy Kaneko

VP, International Sales Stuart Laurence

VP and Creative Director Gaye Allen

VP and Publisher Hannah Rahill

Associate Publisher Amy Marr

Senior Art Director Emma Boys

Associate Editor Donita Boles

Designer Anna Giladi

Photo Manager Meghan Hildebrand

Production Director Chris Hemesath

Color Manager Teri Bell

Production Manager Michelle Duggan

Assistant Food Stylist Lillian Kang

Photographer's Assistants James Thomas,
Brittany Powell, Heidi Ladendorf

Assistant Prop Stylists Daniele Maxwell, Lori Walker